HOW TO
WRITE
NON-FICTION

TURN YOUR KNOWLEDGE
INTO WORDS

Joanna Penn

How to Write Non-Fiction: Turn Your Knowledge Into Words

ISBN: 978-1-912105-78-6

Published by Curl Up Press

Requests to publish work from this book should be sent to:
joanna@CurlUpPress.com

Cover and Interior Design: JD Smith

www.CurlUpPress.com

Contents

Dedicated, with thanks, to all those writers who have impacted my life with their non-fiction books.

Introduction

"Here's the thing: the book that will most change your life is the book you write. The act of writing things down, of justifying your actions, of being cogent and clear and forthright – that's how you change."

Seth Godin

"I can't do this anymore," I sobbed on the phone to my husband from a park just outside the office where I was working. "I can't stand the work. It's so pointless. I feel like I'm wasting my life."

I was working as a business consultant at that time, implementing process change into an entrenched government department. Every day was awful, but that particular day broke me.

"Then leave," Jonathan said. "Do something else with your life. It's not worth it when it makes you so unhappy."

His words struck me, even though we'd discussed it many times before. I was the primary wage-earner in our household, we had a lovely house and all the trappings, and, of course, a mortgage to match. My job paid me well, and I couldn't see a way to escape those golden handcuffs.

So I did what I always did when I was miserable. I went to the bookstore.

I bought a whole load of non-fiction books on how to change your life. *The Success Principles* by Jack Canfield, *The Last Lecture* by Randy Pausch, *The Four Hour Work Week* by Timothy Ferriss. In the days after, I binge-read them all, scribbling notes in my journals along the way. I started listening to audiobooks and podcasts on my commute, and my mindset began to change. I could see a different future.

I talked to my colleagues at work and discovered that most of them were stuck in their jobs too, unhappy but not knowing how to change. I decided that the only way I could help others was to help myself. I would write my own self-help book.

In early 2008, I published *How to Enjoy Your Job or Find a New One*. Catchy title, right!

It didn't set the world on fire, but it certainly changed my life.

That first book directly led to me starting my website, TheCreativePenn.com, in December 2008. It began my journey into learning how to write, publish and market books, and I met other authors and online entrepreneurs along the way. I kept writing and started blogging, podcasting and speaking as I built my creative business on the side.

I left my consulting job in September 2011, the same year my first novel came out. In 2012, I re-wrote and re-issued that first non-fiction book as *Career Change* with new chapters on making the transition from day job to entrepreneur.

At the time of writing this book, I have 27 books out under three different author names. I write non-fiction/self-help as Joanna Penn, thrillers and dark fantasy as J.F.Penn, and co-write sweet contemporary romance as Penny Appleton. I'm an award-nominated, New York Times and USA Today bestseller, an award-winning creative entrepreneur, an international speaker and podcaster, and I run a multi-six-figure business around my writing. These days, I love my work!

All of this came from the decision to write my first non-fiction book. I changed my own life, and since then, I've helped change many more.

A non-fiction book is a powerful thing – but only if you give it your all.

Life is too short to spend time creating something you don't care about. So write your non-fiction book to change your life, to change other people's lives, to tell your story, to touch hearts. We need more of those books in the world. I hope yours will be one of them.

Overview of the book

Part 1 covers the mindset issues that might be stopping you from writing in the first place and how to cope with the rollercoaster of the creative journey.

Part 2 moves into the more practical business aspects of what you need to consider before you write.

Part 3 gets into the actual writing and editing, as well as research, structure, organization and legal issues.

Part 4 is about publishing and product creation, turning your words into various formats that customers can buy.

Part 5 covers marketing for non-fiction books, whether you're just starting out or if you are more established.

You can jump straight to the section that you're interested in, or read the book in order. There are questions, books, and resources throughout the book, and you can download the list with clickable links at:

www.TheCreativePenn.com/nonfictiondownload

* * *

Please note: This book contains some affiliate links to products/services that I recommend and use myself. This means that if you purchase through my links, I receive a small percentage of sale, at no extra cost to you. But of course, there is no obligation to buy or use my links!

Part 1: Before You Write: Mindset

1.1 Why write a non-fiction book?

"Writing isn't about making money, getting famous, getting dates, getting laid, or making friends. In the end, it's about enriching the lives of those who will read your work, and enriching your own life, as well."

Stephen King, On Writing

Writing a book is hard work. You need a reason to carry you through the tough times.

Why do you care about this subject so much that you want to invest the time, emotional energy, and maybe money, in order to write it?

What will keep you going through the process of writing, publishing and marketing?

What is your why?

Here are some of the reasons why people write non-fiction books.

(1) You have been through a particular experience, and you want to help other people going through the same thing

A lot of non-fiction books start this way. I wrote *Career Change* to change my own life, and it continues to help others discover what they really want to do even years later. Sometimes the book that burns on our heart can be the most powerful, our own self-growth manifested in book form.

> "The universe buries strange jewels deep within us all, and then stands back to see if we can find them."
>
> *Elizabeth Gilbert, Big Magic*

(2) You want to build authority, credibility and expert status in a particular field

You want a book to demonstrate authority and thought leadership, augment your business and open doors to speaking and other business or media opportunities. The point of the book is not necessarily to make money in itself but to drive people to your other offerings. This is the 'book as business card' approach.

For example, my book, *How to Make a Living with your Writing*, drives people to my other books and courses. The aim of the book is to provide an introduction to that extended material.

(3) You want to use non-fiction book sales as the basis of your income, so you want to write multiple books in a niche and dominate that market

Although it's unlikely that you will make a million and retire in launch week, some authors do make a full-time living writing only non-fiction, as covered in Part 2.

(4) You have an audience already and write to fulfill their needs, which often coincide with your own interests

I started out writing non-fiction to learn what I needed to know myself about self-publishing and book marketing, and over time, I attracted an audience. Now I write books for that audience and ideas emerge from interacting with my community. For example, *The Successful Author Mindset* came from a blog post that resonated so much, I expanded it into a book.

(5) Writing is how you work out what you think

I often don't know what I think about a subject until I write about it. The writing process is the way I turn my research into reality. I wrote *How to Market a Book* when I was learning about marketing and *Business for Authors: How to be an Author Entrepreneur* as my writing career transitioned into a global business.

"I don't know what I think until I write it down."

Joan Didion

(6) You are deeply fascinated with a topic and want to produce a book on it

These are the type of non-fiction books that can go on to win literary prizes, books that may be commissioned and may consume the author for a long time. One example would be *The Emperor of All Maladies: A Biography of Cancer* by Siddhartha Mukherjee, which won the Pulitzer Prize. Or *Sapiens* by Yuval Noah Harari which I consider one of the most thought-provoking books I've ever read and I recommend to everyone.

Of course, they don't have to be so epic. I've started researching the concept of the shadow for a book that may take me a while to write. I'll get there eventually and in the meantime, I can indulge my love of research and fascination with the topic.

"Nobody is waiting with bated breath for another unknown author to put out another phoned-in book … The real reason to write a book is because there is something you *have* to explore that you think readers want to learn about, not because you think putting 'author' on your LinkedIn profile is smart."

Ryan Holiday, author of Perennial Seller

What's your why?

Whatever the reason behind your desire to write a non-fiction book, I absolutely believe that you should go ahead and write it. After all, the book you write could change your life – as it has done for me. And hopefully, you'll help other people and maybe even make some money along the way!

What is your definition of success?

Your reasons for writing will also relate to your definition of success, which is important to define up front. Otherwise, how will you know when you've achieved it?

You need to get specific here with measurable, time-based goals that will help you mark the journey. For example, how will you measure your goal of achieving authority status in your field? Is it the number of speaking events booked, the number of podcasts you appear on or connecting with a specific influencer in your niche?

What about an income goal?

For some people, making an extra $1000 a month would be a fantastic achievement. For others, you might be aiming for $10,000 a month from turning your book into multiple streams of income. One person's idea of success is rarely the same as another's.

So be specific about how you will measure success – for this book, and for your non-fiction career as an author.

"Writing a book is a tremendous experience. It pays off intellectually. It clarifies your thinking. It builds credibility. It is a living engine of marketing and idea spreading, working every day to deliver your message with authority. You should write one."

Seth Godin

Questions:

- Why are you writing a non-fiction book? What are the reasons that will carry you through the tough times? What is your why?

- What is your definition of success? How will you know when you have achieved it? How will you measure it?

Resources:

- *On Writing: A Memoir of the Craft* – Stephen King

- *Big Magic: Creative Living Beyond Fear* – Elizabeth Gilbert

- Seth Godin's advice for authors: www.sethgodin.typepad.com/seths_blog/2006/08/advice_for_auth.html

- *How to Make a Living with your Writing: Books, Blogging, and More* – Joanna Penn

- *The Successful Author Mindset: A Handbook for Surviving the Writer's Journey* – Joanna Penn

- *Perennial Seller: The Art of Making and Marketing Work That Lasts* – Ryan Holiday

1.2 Can I write a book if I'm not an expert?

"There's no one in the world who can do what
you can do, who can think and see the way you do,
who can create what you can create."

Barbara Sher

I surveyed my audience on The Creative Penn in preparation for this book and asked the question, "What is stopping you from writing?"

Over half of the respondents included some variation of self-doubt and imposter syndrome around whether they would be qualified to write a book. Here are some of their comments:

- Can I write on a topic that I am not an expert in? I sometimes feel like a fraud.

- I don't have the authority to write non-fiction

- I'm not an expert in this field. What right do I have to write this book?

- Do I need a PhD to be taken seriously?

- I don't have the expertise or experience to be an authority on this topic.

- Should I write the book even if I'm not an established professional in my field?

- I have 30 years' experience, but regardless of how much experience I have, self-doubt stops me from writing.

If you feel this way, consider the following.

You can help people wherever you are on the journey

You might have noticed that I am not Malcolm Gladwell … or Elizabeth Gilbert … or any of the other famous non-fiction writers you might like to list.

But I'm an author and I've written eight non-fiction books, so I have experience of the topic of this book. I'm not famous, I don't have a degree in writing or publishing, but I can share my journey and what I've learned along the way.

Perhaps you will even find my experience and advice more relevant *because* I'm not famous, as I'm nearer to where you are on your own author journey. Perhaps something I say will touch you or help you or inspire you, so this book will be value enough.

In the same way, you can write a book based on wherever you are on the journey. Your experience is valuable, and can be shared.

"You are not the only one who feels lost, broken, desperate, joyful, wildly hopeful, yearning or seeking … and you can reassure others who feel the same way."

SARK, Juicy Pens, Thirsty Paper

It's not about you

Of course, the book is all about you in that you write it based on your experience. But on another level, the book is not about you at all.

When it goes out into the world, the book is all about the reader. They read to make their life better and ultimately, they don't care about you. They just want to improve their life or learn something from your writing, or escape their life for a while.

When I decided I needed to give up sugar for health reasons, as discussed in *The Healthy Writer*, I read a whole stack of books from people who had given up sugar. I don't remember any of their names or much about the detail of the books, but I read lots of them over a period of a few weeks, trying to understand how I would feel and gleaning tips and tricks for getting through cravings.

When those authors were writing the books, I'm sure they were obsessing about their lack of credentials, but all I wanted as a reader was their truth, their journey and how it would help me.

You don't have to be 'right.' It's your opinion.

Some writers worry that their book has to be objectively true and correct in every way, and since that's impossible, they don't ever finish the book.

Of course, this will depend on the book you are intending to write. Part 3 covers the importance of research, citations and legal issues around using quotes and copyright material. But don't let the need for exactness paralyze you before you even start.

In *The Healthy Writer*, my co-writer, Dr Euan Lawson, sought out medical studies in peer-reviewed journals to back up his suggestions for healthy practices, but it was our personal anecdotes that impacted people the most.

Many types of non-fiction books are not required to be objectively true. For example, this book is not the definitive guide to writing non-fiction. It can't be, because there are as many ways to write as there are writers and all will have a different take on the subject. But my opinion is valid and hopefully will help you.

Your vulnerability and authenticity will touch people

"The moment that you feel, just possibly, you are walking down the street naked, exposing too much of your heart and your mind, and what exists on the inside, showing too much of yourself...That is the moment you might be starting to get it right."

Neil Gaiman

Another common response in the survey was "Why would people be interested in me?"

In the end, it all comes down to your story and how honestly you share it. Emotion and heart will beat perfect factual prose every time. We are all flawed and our life stories are filled with mistakes and wrong turns, heartache and (hopefully) soaring moments of triumph and joy. Share those and you will touch your reader.

You don't have to be a 'great writer' to write a great book

You do not have to have a degree in writing to be a writer. You do not have to have a college education to write a book that helps people and resonates with them. You don't have to be any good at grammar – you can hire an editor for that.

You DO have to have a passion for sharing your story and lessons learned, and be focused on helping your target market achieve their goals. Be useful, be inspiring, be entertaining, be genuine, and the reader will forgive any foibles in writing.

Who is really an expert anyway?

"Expert: a person who has special skill or knowledge in some particular field; specialist; authority. Possessing special skill or knowledge; trained by practice; skillful or skilled."

Dictionary.com

It's not exactly clear what an expert is. How many degrees do you need? How many years' experience do you need? How many other books should you have read? How do you define skilled?

Language is powerful and our own beliefs about words can keep us in boxes of our own design. You can either go get more degrees and more years of experience, or you can write from where you are now.

You have permission to share your truth

If you're waiting for someone to anoint you with the writer stick, then here you are. You have permission to write your book.

Don't dream of what might be. Get over yourself, go forth, and write!

"Now to have things alive and interesting it must be personal, it must come from the 'I': what I know and feel. For that is the only great and interesting thing. That is the only truth you know, that nobody else does."

Brenda Ueland, If You Want to Write

Questions:

- What's stopping you from writing your book?

- If you think you "need to be an expert," then how do you define expert? How can you become one so you satisfy your own definition?

- Is it possible that other people might call you an expert if you share your journey?

Resources:

- *Juicy Pens, Thirsty Paper: Gifting the World with Your Words and Stories, and Creating the Time and Energy to Actually Do It* – SARK

- *If You Want To Write: A Book About Art, Independence and Spirit* – Brenda Ueland

- *Make Good Art* – Neil Gaiman

1.3 Originality. Or "there are already so many books on the topic"

Every non-fiction gem of wisdom has been said before.

Every story has been written before.

All human experience has already been cataloged in countless books.

These truths can paralyze us, especially in the early days of writing when we don't know how to deal with the demons of self-doubt.

But *your* thoughts have not been written before, and *your* story has not been told before.

You are the original aspect of creativity, and what you bring to the world will be different to what others bring, even on the same topic.

Originality is just a twist on what has already gone before

"Great artists steal."

Pablo Picasso

I read a lot of books on writing before I ever wrote a book and I still read hundreds of books per year on all different kinds of topics. Some I actively read for research, but many others form a psychological milieu that inevitably forms part of my writing process.

When I started writing this book, I brainstormed my table of contents and then bought a whole load of books on writing non-fiction to look for what I might have missed. This kind of intense reading and deconstruction can help you understand the structure of successful books. You can then use what you've learned to put your own spin on the topic.

This is not plagiarism, which is directly copying people's work. It also doesn't mean taking another author's structure and directly reproducing it, changing names and places but keeping the same ideas. It's more about modeling and understanding what works with specific books, noticing what keeps you enthralled as a reader and then using that process in your work.

Whatever you want to write, you need to be aware of the expectations of readers and what has gone before in order to take your book into the realm of something new. There are thousands of books for writers out there, but this book is my experience shared in a way I hope will be useful for you.

So, embrace what has already been written and read widely in the genres you enjoy and want to write in. Elements from those books will resonate in your writing quite naturally, but you can then take them further by bringing in your imagination and your voice.

Don't obsess over perceived imitation or cliché in a first draft. Just get the words down and as you self-edit, go through and fix it up.

"The older I get, the less impressed I become
with originality. These days, I'm far more moved by
authenticity. Attempts at originality can often feel
forced and precious, but authenticity has quiet
resonance that never fails to stir me."

Elizabeth Gilbert, Big Magic

Questions:

- What are some of the top books in your genre, or top authors, that you can look at modeling?

- How are those other books a development on earlier books in the field?

- What can you learn from them and expand on to include in your own book?

Resources:

- *Steal Like An Artist: 10 Things Nobody Told You About Being Creative* – Austin Kleon

- *Big Magic: Creative Living Beyond Fear* – Elizabeth Gilbert

1.4 Who are you? Personal stories and your writer's voice

"Writers end up writing about their obsessions. Things that haunt them; things they can't forget; stories they carry in their bodies waiting to be released."

Natalie Goldberg, Writing Down the Bones

Readers expect to know something about you when they read a book. In fact, they may only pick it up if you can demonstrate that you're the right person to learn from.

You don't have to be THE expert on a particular topic, just one or two steps ahead of your target market. In fact, it can be better if you are closer to the reader's experience.

I wrote *Career Change* when I was still stuck in my day job, and updated it once I had changed my life in the way I'd written about. I'm glad I wrote *Business for Authors* when I was just starting out with my author business, going through the nitty gritty questions of things like bank accounts and international tax. Now these things are second nature and I am less in touch with the challenges of starting a creative business. Although, of course, I still have the challenge of running one!

Why are you the right person for this book?

"You own everything that happened to you.
Tell your stories."

Anne Lamott, Bird by Bird

Lots of people write about the same topics – but your experiences make your book original. It's your take on the subject. You have to trust yourself and lean into what makes you YOU.

Brainstorm aspects of your life that might be more inter-esting to other people than it is to you. For example, I discovered that my English accent goes down well with Americans. It doesn't make me special in the UK, but it really stands out on US-based podcasts, and I frequently tell my story of escaping my life as corporate cubicle slave to become a full-time author entrepreneur.

- What's interesting about your background that will help you stand out?

- What part of your story will help illustrate the topic you want to talk about?

The more you share your personal story, the more people will resonate with your book. If people begin to know you, like you and trust you, they will be more likely to listen to you and buy your books and products. Of course, you have to define your boundaries, but personal stories are so important – both in the book itself and also in your marketing.

As Maya Angelou said, "People will forget what you said, people will forget what you did, but people will never forget how you made them feel." Emotion comes from story and connection, not from listing facts or prescriptive How-To information.

Finding your voice as a non-fiction author

"I write non-fiction in this thriller-esque style. I have all the facts; I research it. I have thousands of pages of court documents … I try to get inside my stories."

Ben Mezrich, author of The Accidental Millionaires: The Founding of Facebook, which was turned into the Oscar-winning film, The Social Network

I hope you can hear my voice as you read this book. If you've listened to one of my podcasts or watched my videos on YouTube, then you should be able to tell that this is really me. I'm not putting on a specific tone to write this book. I'm just using my natural form of expression. My words. My voice.

But my writing certainly didn't start out this way.

I used to work as a business consultant, implementing Accounts Payable into large and small companies. I wrote process documentation and technical specifications, as well as training material for the system. Not the most creative work, and all written with no personality, no voice. It took me years of blogging before I relaxed and could write as I talk.

People connect with people, and they want some indication of your journey and who you are, even in a prescriptive How-To book. You can write with authority, but still be friendly and authentic. In an age of increasing automation, and particularly journalism and non-fiction written by AI bots, it's only your voice that will help you stand out.

If you come from an academic background or have spent years writing dry business documents, you may find writing in a more natural voice difficult. That's okay. Just write the first draft and edit it later.

When I co-wrote *The Healthy Writer* with Dr Euan Lawson, he wrote his initial chapters in the same tone as his medical journal articles. They cited medical studies with no personal opinion or experience. Once I explained that we were writing a self-help book for a general audience of writers, Euan started using dictation to write his first drafts, weaving personal stories and opinions around the medical evidence, which brought the book alive. We also removed any technical jargon and made it as easy to read as possible.

Read through some of the non-fiction books that you resonate with in your niche. What kind of voice does the author have?

"Don't write a book that's a regurgitation of someone else's work. Be the authority that provides lasting value to the reader."

Steve Scott, How to Write a Non-Fiction Book in 21 days – That Readers Love!

Questions:

- Brainstorm aspects of your life that might be more interesting to other people than it is to you.

- What's interesting about your background that will help you stand out?

- What part of your story will help you illustrate the topic you want to talk about?

- How will you set boundaries for privacy but also share authentically?

- Read through some of the books you resonate with in your niche. What kind of voice does the author use?

Resources:

- *How to Write a Non-Fiction Book in 21 days – That Readers Love!* – Steve Scott

- *Writing Down the Bones: Freeing the Writer Within* – Natalie Goldberg

- *Bird by Bird: Some Instructions on Writing and Life* – Anne Lamott

1.5 Fear and self-doubt

"If writers had to wait until their precious psyches were completely serene, there wouldn't be much writing done."

William Styron

Writing is as much of a mind game as it is the discipline of getting words on the page. Fear and self-doubt are part of the creative process, and successful writers learn to live with them and create anyway.

I've covered this in detail in *The Successful Author Mindset: A Handbook for Surviving the Writer's Journey*, so this is just an overview of the most common mindset issues that writers face and that you might encounter on the journey.

Self-doubt

My writing is terrible. I just can't seem to get what's in my head onto the page. I feel like a fraud. I'll never be as good as X writer so I might as well give up.

Fear of failure

What if I don't get an agent or a publisher? What if I self-publish and no one buys it? What if no one likes my book? What if I tell everyone I'm writing a book and then I never finish it? What if I don't make any money and it's all a waste of time?

Fear of rejection and criticism

What if an editor rips the book apart with red ink? What if I get one-star reviews? What if I get slated by the critics? What if the criticism is true and I really am that bad?

Fear of judgment

What will people think of what I write? What if they think I'm weird for writing this? What if my family and friends hate what I've written?

Fear of success

What if my book is a runaway success and suddenly everyone knows who I am and then trolls attack me on social media? What if my accounts get hacked, or people ask me for money?

These experiences are part of the rollercoaster creative journey, and we all go through aspects of them along the way. So you are not alone if you feel this way.

Fear is often worse than the reality

Your wonderful mind is trying to protect you. It is conjuring possible threats and helping you avoid them. But we have all faced fears only to find that they are not the monsters of our imagination.

No one is going to die if you write your book and it only sells five copies. No one is going to die if you get a one-star review. And the only person who will care if you don't finish your book is you.

So finish it and face those fears. You'll likely find they are unfounded. And if they do happen, then write about it in your next book and move on.

Embrace these fears as part of the creative process

Be encouraged by the fact that virtually all other creatives, including your writing heroes, feel these things too with every book they write. In fact, if you don't feel any kind of doubt or fear, perhaps you don't care enough about your book.

When you feel fear and self-doubt, acknowledge it. Write down your feelings in your journal ... and then continue with your writing.

Protect yourself in practical ways

There are ways to deal with some of these fears in a practical manner. Use professional editors to make sure your book is a fantastic finished product. Check chapter 3.14 on legal issues if you're worried about getting sued or revealing too much about people who are alive. If you are writing something that might shock your loved ones or your community, then consider using a pseudonym, as covered in chapter 2.6.

If you're concerned about people finding you online, then make sure you have gone through your privacy settings on social media and your website. Be clear on your boundaries and how much you are willing to share about your personal life and then stick to them. Find a supportive community of people who understand the creative process.

Once you have dealt with things on a pra
blocks will only be in your mind. So get ba

Return to your why

Why are you writing this book? Why do you care enough to spend your time and effort working on this project? What drives you?

If you are still not sure, go back to chapter 1.1 and work through the possible reasons. Then write your why on a sticky note and put it by your desk. Look at it whenever you feel like giving up, or when fear and doubt batter you. Take a deep breath and get back to the blank page.

Questions:

- What are some of your fears and doubts? Identifying them is half the battle!

- What can you put in place to help you manage when the rollercoaster gets too much?

- What is your 'why' that will help you through difficult times?

Resources:

- *The Successful Author Mindset: A Handbook for Surviving the Writer's Journey* – Joanna Penn

- *Art and Fear: Observations on the Perils (and Rewards) of Artmaking* – David Bayles and Ted Orland

1.6 The day a non-fiction book changed my life

As we move into the next part of the book, I want to return to the question of why we write. Fundamentally, we write to change lives – our own and other people's. Here's a moment in my life that pivoted on a non-fiction book.

There are moments in our lives where a decision changes everything. That moment may be out of our control, or it may be a conscious choice, but when life forks in such a significant way, the opposite path becomes the road not taken, a parallel life.

* * *

Bali, 2008

I tucked a frangipani flower behind my ear and lay back on the recliner, looking up at the blue sky. The air smelled of jacaranda and lime leaf. Birds sang in the palm trees and in the distance, I could hear the putt-putt of local scooters. Jonathan swam in the pool in front of me, his strokes making a light splash as he moved through the water. We'd been out walking along the waterfront earlier, looking out across the ocean where we planned to scuba dive later in the week. For now, we relaxed by the pool with a cocktail as the bright day turned to a balmy evening.

Our week in Bali was a late honeymoon after our wedding in Australia attended by our very international family. It was also a turning point for me. I was planning to come off my contraceptive pill on this trip. I was 33, and we'd been talking about starting a family. We had a house with extra bedrooms. We had stable jobs. And now, we were in paradise ... so why was I hesitating?

I pushed my concerns aside and picked up the book I'd found at the airport. *Eat, Pray, Love* by Elizabeth Gilbert. Everyone was talking about it, and the story was partially set in Ubud, a town in the hills north from where we were staying. I started to read, and in the next ten minutes, my life changed as I read her words.

"I couldn't stop thinking about what my sister had said to me once, as she was breast-feeding her firstborn: 'Having a baby is like getting a tattoo on your face. You really need to be certain it's what you want before you commit.'"

Elizabeth talked about her excitement at future travel, and that if she couldn't be as excited about having a baby as she was about booking her next trip, then she really shouldn't be having one.

I put the book down, even though I was only in the opening chapters. I recognized myself in those words, and it shocked me. I looked down at Jonathan in the pool, calmly swimming lengths, and wondered if our new marriage would survive the conversation we desperately needed to have.

* * *

Whatever your feelings about having children, I hope you can respect my choice – and my husband's. Because the subsequent conversation revealed that we were both feeling the same way, we had just assumed the other one was so sure that considering a different path wasn't possible. And yet now, we're ten years happily married and happily child-free – by choice.

This is not a discussion on the pros and cons of having children. It is a book about writing your story to help yourself, but also to help others. Elizabeth Gilbert's memoir told *her* truth and yet it connected with me across time and space. Her words resonated and gave me permission to feel what I thought was taboo.

I don't know why I needed permission, but I did. I'm a good girl, always have been. I want people to like me. I want approval. I wanted to be the perfect daughter, the perfect daughter-in-law, the perfect wife, the perfect mother. By actively making the decision to be child-free, I would be none of those things.

But I would be living the life of my choice.

So, please don't write just another book filled with prescriptive 'How To' information. Write your truth. It might change your life and touch the hearts of those who desperately need to hear it.

Part 2: Before you Write: Business

2.1 Types of non-fiction books

It's important to consider up front what type of book you're writing. There are some broad types of books that will help you start to shape your own. These sit above genre or sub-category in the bookstore and of course, some will span multiple types.

The important thing is to identify where your book might fit in the ecosystem and find some examples for you to model with your book. Go through your bookshelf. What are the books you like and why? Where do they fit?

Here are some of the main types of non-fiction book.

Clear transformation for the reader. How To / Instructional books

This includes the broad categories of Self-Help, Art and Photography, Business & Investing, Cooking & Food, Crafts & Hobbies, Health & Fitness & Dieting, Sports and Travel.

It's easy to identify a target market and the reader may not even care that much about who wrote the book. For example, *How to Cook Simple Healthy Meals for Kids with a Slow Cooker*. Do you care who wrote this? If you just got a slow cooker and you want some help with ideas for meals for your kids, you'd buy it.

Motivational books like *The Success Principles: How to Get From Where You Are To Where You Want To Be* by Jack Canfield, or *How to Practice: The Way to a Meaningful Life* by the Dalai Lama, also fit into this niche. My books fit here, too.

Books in these niches can be evergreen so although it can be easy to write for them, older works may dominate the category, and it can be hard to stand out. For example, under Job Hunting, you will still find *What Color is your Parachute?* by Richard N Bolles, first published in 1972 and still updated every year. However, if you search for *Career Change*, you will find my book there, ten years after publication.

This is likely to be the type of book that you're writing and the type I'll be focusing on the most as it lends itself most easily to a creative business model.

Inspirational/personal stories / memoir / narrative non-fiction

"There's a difference between writing non-fiction to show-case a business (as a calling card) and writing heart-based non-fiction to teach deep wisdom."

Dr Karen Wyatt, from The Creative Penn survey

These books are far more about the personal journey that an individual goes through and can help the reader by providing inspiration as well as an example of overcoming a challenge.

I read a lot of these books when I decided to give up sugar. For example, *I Quit Sugar* by Sarah Wilson and *Year of No*

Sugar: A Memoir by Eve Schaub, are quite different books to *The Case Against Sugar* by Gary Taubes, which fits in the category below. Prescriptive information is useful, but the personal story of transformation can be more motivating.

Other examples include *Eat, Pray, Love* by Elizabeth Gilbert, a memoir about finding happiness after a painful divorce, but could also be compared to books in the category above like *The Happiness Project* by Gretchen Rubin, which still has personal anecdotes but also more prescriptive How-To information as well.

Narrative non-fiction, also known as creative non-fiction, uses more overt storytelling to engage the reader in the book and perhaps has more in common with an engaging documentary film. It's essentially true but still feels like an entertainment experience rather than a lecture. Examples include *The Big Short* by Michael Lewis, which was turned into an Oscar-winning film, as well as *The Immortal Life of Henrietta Lacks* by Rebecca Skloot.

Topic-based evergreen books

These are books read for informational purposes and are often evergreen. They are written for the mass market as opposed to academic tomes. For example, a biography like *Steve Jobs* by Walter Isaacson, a social science book like *Sapiens* by Yuval Noah Harari, a finance book like *Money, Master the Game* by Tony Robbins, or a history book like *Guns, Germs and Steel* by Jared Diamond.

Shawn Coyne, author of *The Story Grid*, calls these Big Idea books and explains why they can be so successful:

"Academics appreciate the research cited to support the Big Idea. How-To readers take away actionable steps that they believe can better their lives. And Narrative non-fiction readers are captivated by the storytelling. This is why Big publishers love the Big Idea book ... it can become a block-buster bestseller."

Academic textbooks / technological / trends / manuals

Books in this niche have a specific audience e.g. universities, schools, libraries, or specific industry professionals. They can attract higher prices per unit, and they can sell in bulk, so are generally not even measured by bestseller lists. They often need to be regularly updated to stay current, so there are frequently multiple editions over time.

The need to update material regularly can be difficult for the author and this can become a rat race of content updates if you have more than one book. For example, if you write a book on Facebook marketing, it will likely be out of date on the day of publication, as they change the algorithm regularly and what worked last week, might not work this week. The same applies to software or hardware books, as well as medical, legal, technological shifts, or anything written in a field where advances are made on a regular basis.

It's also applicable for political books that fit a zeitgeist. For example, the British Brexit vote gave rise to a new political sub-genre of books, but change continues daily. The same could apply to the Trump administration in the US. If the political shift becomes more of a cultural movement, the books could be evergreen, a moment of personal experience in an ever-changing environment. But it's certainly worth considering shelf-life when you're looking at book topics for a long-term career.

Questions:

- What kind of book do you want to write?

- Can you identify 5-10 books that your book will be similar to? Which categories do they sit in? Where do they fit in the ecosystem?

Resources:

- Shawn Coyne on The Story Grid blog. Breakdown of non-fiction genres: www.storygrid.com/ nonfictions-big-genre-silos

- *The Story Grid: What Good Editors Know* – Shawn Coyne

2.2 Business models for non-fiction books

"It often takes longer than you think to turn an idea into a money-making business."

Elaine Pofeldt, The Million Dollar, One-Person Business

Many non-fiction authors have creative or income goals that go beyond the book, so it's important to cover the various business models up front so you can incorporate them into your process as you write.

This chapter is for you if you want to make money around your book. It is less relevant for those writing more personal stories like memoir or academic books, or where the author is not concerned about making money at all.

Here are the most common business models for non-fiction authors.

(1) Make money from book sales and licensing only

You *can* make a full-time income from just book sales, but you need to have a high production model with multiple books aimed at a hungry audience so you can sell lots of them. Because, let's face it, a book is a low-priced product and you have to sell in high volumes to make decent money.

A great example of this model is Joseph Alexander, who has a series of books on playing the guitar. It's a great niche, combining his passion and skill with an audience who want to learn to play. He has books on types of music, like rock, jazz or blues; then books aimed at beginners, e.g. *First Chord Progressions* moving through to advanced topics like *Sightreading Mastery*. In this way, he can dominate the niche and readers who find one of his books are likely to go on and buy more.

Another example is S.J.Scott, who writes multiple books in the self-help habits niche. Both these writers are independent and make a full-time living from book sales.

This model includes expanding formats into ebooks, print, workbooks, audiobooks, and bundling, as well as translation, licensing international territories, and exploiting subsidiary rights like film/TV/media/gaming, which I'll cover more in Part 4 on publishing. It also means selling direct from your website, as well as through the distributors.

(2) Book as lead-generation for physical products, courses, consulting, services, webinars, software or affiliate products

In this business model, the book leads people into the author's ecosystem and results in sales of higher priced products and services. These may be the author's own, or link to affiliate products where the author receives a commission on the sale. This is the most common strategy for non-fiction authors in the self-help/business/marketing niches and why some consider the book more as a marketing tool than as income.

One mega example would be Tony Robbins, who started out with books, audio programs and live events and now runs a multi-million dollar self-help empire. I recommend the Netflix documentary *I Am Not Your Guru* if you want to see behind the scenes of his live events. His books lead into products, experiences and services.

Other examples include Russell Brunson, who used *DotCom Secrets* to sell his software. Sophia Amoruso used her book, *GirlBoss,* as PR for her online store, Nasty Gal, and Netflix did a series based on her story. Mark McGuinness, poet and creative coach, writes books on productivity and resilience as a way into his free email course, podcast and premium coaching for creative entrepreneurs.

A single book can be the basis for a business that lasts a long time. Look at Julia Cameron, who wrote *The Artist's Way* over 25 years ago. She spun that off into variations on the original book, plus she has video courses, events, and workbooks.

For services, look at Bryan Cohen's book, *How to Write a Sizzling Synopsis*, which is a super-useful book for authors who want to write their own back-of-the-book blurbs, but also acts as a way into Best Page Forward, Bryan's synopsis writing business.

I use this model, too. My free ebook, *Successful Self-Publishing,* has affiliate links to products and services that I promote, and this book also leads into a multi-media course on how to write non-fiction.

Even if you give away the farm in your book, people will want to hire you to do it for them or buy your other books, products or services.

(3) Book as the basis of a speaking career

Most speakers have one or more books, and they often base their speaking topics around the book. It acts as credibility that they know their topic and also as a business card to get more speaking work.

In terms of income, a speaker might include copies of their book as part of their speaking fee, or sell them at the back of the room as a lower priced product with courses and consulting and other events as an up-sell.

Robert McKee performs his non-fiction book *Story* at multi-day events aimed at writers and filmmakers. He also has *Storynomics,* a class and now a book aimed at corporates who want to integrate story into marketing.

Amy Schmittauer, author of *Vlog Like a Boss*, speaks on video marketing. Chris Ducker, author of *Rise of the Youpreneur*, speaks on how to build a business around a personal brand.

There are also introvert speakers who have used books as part of their talks. Examples include Malcolm Gladwell, Brené Brown, and Susan Cain who wrote the brilliant *Quiet: The Power of Introverts in a World That Can't Stop Talking*.

Whatever your personality type, you can use your book/s as part of a speaking career. If you do identify as an introvert and want to be a speaker, then check out my book, *Public Speaking for Authors, Creatives and Other Introverts*.

(4) Bulk sales and special sales

"These cash mines are all around you, but until
now you have probably overlooked them, because unlike
bookstores, they do not have canyons of bookshelves.
Instead, these non-trade sales outlets are disguised as
corporations, associations, home shopping networks,
book clubs, schools, catalogs, gift shops, retail stores,
government agencies, military bases, supermarkets,
drug stores, and so many more."

Brian Jud, How to Make Real Money Selling Books
(Without Worrying About Returns)

This is one of those business models that you don't hear about much, because books sold in bulk are not measured by any of the bestseller lists. So a book might sell millions of copies and never make the bestseller lists, but the author will be doing very well indeed!

The aim of this model is to write a book that appeals to a certain market, for example, a book on looking after your dog might sell to pet stores, or a pet food company. Then develop relationships with your target market, pitching your book to bulk buy or use in a special promotion. They might even do a branded print run with the name of their company on it.

Business book *Who Moved My Cheese*, by Spencer Johnson and Kenneth Blanchard was bought in bulk by companies all over the US to give to employees and still remains a classic.

Author and executive coach, Honorée Corder, does this with her book, *The Successful Single Mom,* which she licenses to attorneys to give to their clients when going through a divorce.

"One of the ways that I sell my books is I let companies and firms do ... custom printing where they take the back cover and make it a brochure about their business. It's really a marketing tool for law firms and certified divorce, financial advisors, those types of people. They'll buy the book in quantity and put their information on the back."

Combine all the models to create multiple streams of income

These are the most common business models for author-entrepreneurs and you can, of course, mix and match between them. I use aspects of the first three in my business, which I cover in more detail in *How to Make a Living with your Writing.*

As an overview, my non-fiction income streams include:

- **Book sales income** from ebook, print, audiobook, workbook formats, from multiple stores, and from 89 countries (mostly in English).

- Sales of **my own multi-media courses**

- **Affiliate income** from referring products and services I use and recommend

- **Sponsorship and advertising** based on my podcast and YouTube channel, which started out as a way to market my books but have now turned into income streams

- Professional **speaking** income

Design your ecosystem around the book

If you consider your business model up front, you can design an eco-system around the book in advance to maximize your revenue and opportunities.

Of course, you do need to think of the book with a business mindset. There are some who use the 'book as baby' metaphor, but I much prefer the 'book as employee.' You're going to have an initial period of growing, nurturing and development, but once that book is out in the world, then it should earn its keep, and designing an ecosystem around it will help do that for the long term.

A 'funnel' is a way to direct your readers through a journey with you, preferably through your books, services and other products, so that they are a happy customer and you make a decent return. The book acts as a way into the funnel, an entry point into your ecosystem.

An example might be a non-fiction book, which acts as your authority for a speaking platform, a small income stream and lead-generation for other products. The book offers readers a specific audio/video/ebook download if they sign up for an email list on your website.

Within the useful series of emails, there are video tutorials which lead into a premium multi-media course, and/or a monthly membership site for recurring revenue. There are also emails within the series that offer other products and services that the author uses personally and is an affiliate for, as well as premium one-on-one consulting. The book also leads to professional speaking engagements at premium rates. Hence, multiple income streams from one product.

Questions:

- Do you want to create income from your book? If yes, which business model are you interested in?

- Think of some of the authors you like. Go to their websites and look at the different ways they make an income. How can you model them?

- How could you plan your ecosystem to make the most of the material you are creating?

Resources:

- *The Million Dollar, One-Person Business: Make Great Money. Work the Way You Like. Have the Life you Want* – Elaine Pofeldt

- *How to Make a Living with your Writing: Books, Blogging, and More* – Joanna Penn

- *Business for Authors: How to be an Author Entrepreneur* – Joanna Penn

- *The Business of Being a Writer* – Jane Friedman

- *How to Make Real Money Selling Books (Without Worrying About Returns)* – Brian Jud

- *Public Speaking for Authors, Creatives and Other Introverts* – Joanna Penn

- *You Must Write a Book: Boost Your Brand, Get More Business, and Become The Go-To Expert* – Honorée Corder

2.3 Who is your book for? Identify your target market

"Niche is the new mainstream."

James Watt, Business for Punks

Most authors writing their first book think that it's for everyone.

But it's not.

You have to hone in on who your book is really for. Because people are not buying your book. **They're buying the promise of transformation.** They're buying an escape from reality, a way out of their current situation, whether that is a moment of traveling in another person's shoes or specific steps on how to change.

The reader cares about their own situation and how you can help them through education, inspiration or entertainment. Here are some of the questions you want to consider:

- What are the problems that your target market has? What are their burning questions?

- What are their challenges and fears? What's holding them back? How are you going to help them?

- What are the benefits to these specific readers?

- What is the promise you are making with this book?

- What transformation will they have by the end of the book? How do you want them to change?

- How narrow can you make your target market?

Put yourself in the mind of the reader

Why do people read non-fiction? How does that relate to your idea?

They want an **answer to a specific problem**. This explains the popularity of weight loss and self-help books every January. What specific problem will your book solve?

They are interested in a **specific topic** and buy lots of books in that niche. I have a lot of books on writing, and most likely, so do you! What sub-categories does your book fit into on the online bookstores and is this a niche that people are buying lots of books in?

They like the writer. This is why those with a large platform get book deals. Just check out books by YouTubers, Instagrammers, celebrities, and anyone with a big enough blog or podcast or TED talk. If you have an audience, you can get a book deal because people will buy and read it anyway. Do you have an audience already? What do they want from you?

These questions will help you define your target market, your ideal reader.

If you already have an author platform, a blog, podcast, speaking or other business, then you will already know who your readers are, but for many non-fiction writers, a consideration of audience comes *after* the book is written and they are wondering how to market it. But **understanding who your reader is in advance of writing will help a lot**, and any time spent on it now will help later on.

Demographics and psychographics

You can start with demographics, things like gender, age, race, socio-economic status, country. For example, women aged 25-40 who live in small-town USA with young children. Or single men aged 25-35 who live in Silicon Valley and have technical jobs that leave them with more money than time.

Some books are obviously aimed at demographics, for example, *What to Expect When You're Expecting* by Heidi Murkoff is a classic book for pregnant women. When I went to have a look at it on Amazon, the next recommended book was *What to Expect When your Wife is Expanding* by Thomas Hill, clearly aimed at husbands/partners of pregnant women. A clever demographic switch.

Psychographics are more related to aspects of personality. For example, my book *Public Speaking for Authors, Creatives and other Introverts* is aimed at a psychographic. It doesn't matter what your gender, race, or age – if you are an introvert author/creative and you need to do some public speaking, then this book is for you.

Another example is *Rich Dad, Poor Dad* by Robert Kiyosaki, which is for people who want to learn about money, and I've met people of all demographics who started their financial education with that book.

You can also consider where the reader is on their journey. Are they a beginner or an expert? For example, *A Begin-*

ner's *Guide to Cryptocurrency Investing* and *Advanced Crypto Futures* are two different books within the same area. Stages of life also apply, for example, *Time Management for Students in Grad School* vs. *Time Management for Busy Mums* vs. *Making the Most of your Grandkids and Still Having Time for Holidays.*

If you're still struggling, consider who your book is NOT for or what you won't cover in the material. For example, this book is not aimed at people who want to write a novel. I have a different book coming for that!

"Don't try to sell your book to everyone … Far better to obsess about a little subset of the market – that subset that you have permission to talk with, that subset where you have credibility, and most important, that subset where people just can't live without your book."

Seth Godin, Advice for Authors

You are your reader.
You are not your reader.

It's a paradox, I know, but in many ways, you are your reader because you will generally want to write a book because of a problem you've faced, or a challenge you've personally overcome.

But in other ways, you are *not* your reader, because your demographics might be completely different, and the very act of writing and finishing a book will set you apart, since most people never achieve that goal.

So keep yourself in mind, but don't fixate on readers having to be exactly the same as you.

Research other books in your niche

Writers are readers, so what are the 5-10 books that your book will be like? What can you discover about the target market from how those books are packaged? What do the titles and covers have in common? Why are you attracted to those books?

In what way will your book be similar to those other books? In what way will it be different?

What if there are no other books in your niche?

If you are writing in an emerging area, then there may well be no books in your niche. For example, books on cryptocurrency and Blockchain have boomed in the last year, but were practically non-existent before that. On a smaller example, when I wrote *Business for Authors: How to be an Author Entrepreneur*, there were no other books on business for authors, as it was generally assumed that agents or publishers did all that stuff for you. Now there are lots of them as authors take control of their own creative careers.

But – and it is a big but – it's much easier to sell books to an existing market! It's easier to identify readers and you'll have better category and keyword choices, as well as books and authors to target with advertising.

So really look at your niche. Could you use different words in your title to make it fit better into an existing niche or are you truly blazing a trail into a new area?

How big is your niche?

You can make a judgment about the size of your niche by using a number of different tools to gauge interest in books like yours.

Go to Amazon and browse through the top-selling books in the categories you're interested in. There will be a ranking per category and also an overall ranking in the Kindle or Books store. The lower the number, the more books it's selling.

For example, at the time of writing, Marie Kondo's *The Life-Changing Magic of Tidying Up* is #23 in Cleaning, Caretaking and Relocating (yes, that is a category!) and #26,061 in the overall Kindle store. The #1 book in that category is *Emergency Food Storage and Survival Handbook* by Peggy Layton which is at #803 in the entire Kindle store. So this looks like a category that sells pretty well.

You can also check the reports on **K-lytics** for the top genres, as well as more granular data you can download in order to check the sub-categories.

KDP Rocket gives you the ability to see what particular books are earning and search by keyword for other ideas.

Google Adword tools and other keyword tools will give you the number of searches per month. As I describe further in chapter 2.5 on book titles, I used this method to change the title of my first book to *Career Change*, which resulted in a lot more organic sales as people were searching for it.

Is it worth writing in a small niche?

If you have identified a small niche for your target market, is it still worth writing the book? In the survey conducted for this book, many asked this question.

In my opinion, it is always worth it to write – *if* you care about the topic.

There is no point in spending your precious time on a project that you only write for commercial reasons unless you can be sure of making money on it.

But if you're writing from the heart about a topic you care about, about something that changes your life in the process of writing it, then it's absolutely worth it.

Ideally, you will now have some idea of who your target market is. But you don't need to have it exactly mapped out yet, you can hone it as you work through the process of writing.

Questions:

- What are the problems that your target market has? What are their burning questions?

- What are their challenges and fears? What's holding them back? How are you going to help them?

- What are the benefits to these specific readers?

- What is the promise you are making with this book?

- What transformation will they have by the end of the book? How do you want them to change?

- How narrow can you make your target market?

- Do you have an idea of the size of your niche?

- What are the 5-10 books that your book will be like?

- What can you discover about the target market from how those books are packaged? What do the titles and covers have in common? Why are you attracted to those books?

- In what way will your book be similar to those other books? In what way will it be different?

Resources:

- *Business for Punks: Break All the Rules – The Brewdog Way* - James Watt

- Seth Godin. Advice for authors: www.sethgodin.typepad.com/seths_blog/2006/08/advice_for_auth.html

- K-lytics genre/niche reports: www.TheCreativePenn.com/genre

- KDP Rocket for category and keyword research: www.TheCreativePenn.com/rocket

2.4 Decide on the topic for your book

"Write on subjects in which you have enough interest on your own to see you through all the stops, starts, hesitations, and other impediments along the way."

John McPhee, Draft No. 4

Hopefully, you will already have some idea of the broad topic you want to write about, but now you need to get more specific. Here are some things to take into consideration.

Top-down or bottom-up writing

There are two main ways to decide on the specific topic of your book. The 'top-down' approach is deciding on an area that you care about and then thinking about the audience later. This is the most common way for new authors to write, as the first book is usually based on a burning desire to share an experience.

I wrote *Career Change* because I wanted to understand how I could find work I enjoyed. I felt my life was wasted in my meaningless corporate job, so I wrote that first book to fix my life and hopefully help others. But I certainly didn't have an existing audience, and I didn't do any research on who they might be or consider how I would reach them.

The 'bottom-up' approach is looking at your target market or existing audience, and shaping the book to serve their needs. This should still relate to a topic you're interested in and have experience with, but it intersects with a market who want it.

I wrote *The Successful Author Mindset* because a blog post on the emotional rollercoaster of being a writer attracted so many comments and social shares that I knew I had to look into it more. The book emerged from a need I saw in myself and my audience and addresses the common feelings of self-doubt, fear of failure, writer's block, and much more. That book continues to sell every month, and it's also the book I get the most emails about, so it continues to help my audience, too.

Write what you know – or write what you're interested in

You'll most likely have some idea of the broader aspects of your book. Maybe you're already a speaker on corporate communications, maybe you've discovered a diet that works for you, or perhaps you have a deep interest in military history. You already know about your chosen topic, so that's what you'll write about.

Everyone has some area of experience or expertise, something they know more about than other people. Even if it seems trivial to you, it can still be interesting and useful to others, and you will be one step ahead of those just starting out.

Or perhaps you're interested in writing about a subject you want to learn about and research. All these starting points are valid, but now you need to narrow the topic down further.

Evergreen vs. time-specific

One of the issues with non-fiction is that it can age – especially if you're writing a book on a fast-moving technological, political or scientific topic, or even an area where trends shift consumer behavior. Non-fiction that ages like this may need to be updated, at least every couple of years, but more regularly if necessary.

Evergreen topics can remain popular for years and may never need updating, so keep that in mind as you decide on your book.

Research your niche in the bookstores

You want to spend time writing something you love, but you'd also like to make some money. So, the big question for non-fiction is how to find the intersection between something you care about and commercial viability.

Start by identifying 5-10 books that are similar to what you want to write, or at least are targeted to the same audience if you haven't done this already.

Search for those books on Amazon and then look at the sub-categories they sit within. You can then click into those sub-categories and find other books that are in the same niche.

- What do you like about the book?
- What don't you like?
- What is the expectation of the reader?

- What problem is the book solving?

- What could you do differently?

These questions should help you narrow down the specific topic you want to tackle in the book as well as your target market. To expand on my earlier examples, the more specific topics might be:

- Employee engagement: How to communicate with employees and drive your business to success. Aimed at CEOs and corporate managers.

- Easy gluten-free and vegan dieting for weight loss and health. Aimed at busy women who have struggled with other diets and can't spend a long time in the kitchen preparing food.

- Modern military history of the USA. Aimed at men who buy in the Military history category and intended to be the first in a series on military history.

Write to market

Think like a publisher, rather than an author.

- What would be the best way to make money from a book?

- What will make it worth the time and investment?

- Can you find an existing audience and write to please them?

This is why you get so many miracle diet books in January and beach-body diet books in the summer. The Health & Wellness niche is huge, and someone who buys one diet book will often buy a ton of them! Or perhaps you're like me and own 100+ books on various aspects of writing, and you're always looking for that next book to take you one step further.

Writing to market is more common for established writers who have already written the book of their heart and are now looking for other income streams.

You can find hungry markets by looking at the Amazon categories and then looking at the ranking of the top-selling books. If they are less than 20,000 overall in the store, those books sell a decent amount of copies.

Here are three examples of rankings current at the time of writing.

Kindle eBooks > Crafts, Hobbies & Home > Crafts & Hobbies > Knitting

The number 1 book is #4651 in the store

The number 20 book is at #75,264

Compare that to:

Kindle eBooks > Crafts, Hobbies & Home > Crafts & Hobbies > Book Making & Binding

The number 1 book is at #38,820 in the store

The number 20 book is at #481,022

Compare that to:

Kindle eBooks > Business & Money > Entrepreneurship & Small Business > Entrepreneurship

The number 1 book is at #95 in the store

The number 20 book is at #6413

Which niche sells the most books?

Hopefully, you can tell that the Entrepreneurship niche has the hungriest market, with Knitting next, followed by Book Making. However, Entrepreneurship is also more competitive, and the top-selling books are often big name bloggers or speakers with traditional publishing, so some of the smaller niches might be more appropriate.

It's definitely worth getting to know the niche you want to publish in, as this will help you with ideas for other books to read for research, as well as book titles and cover design options and marketing ideas for later.

Use free writing

In some cases, you might not know exactly what you want to write. Perhaps you have too many ideas and don't know which one to focus on. Perhaps you're afraid to commit to one topic as you have so many varied interests. Perhaps you can't figure out your main message.

If you're struggling, then try using free writing to work through it all. Set a timer for 20 minutes and then write without stopping, without censorship, without self-judgment, without over-thinking.

Don't stop writing until the timer goes off. You can use your various ideas as prompts, or just write what's in your mind. Do this every day for a few weeks, and you will find something emerges as your primary idea.

Then settle on one topic and move forward with that. Chapter 3.8 goes into focus and 'shiny object syndrome' if you're still struggling.

Questions:

- What specific niche topic are you going to write about?

- Which sub-categories does this fit into in the bookstores?

- If you haven't yet done so, list 5-10 books that are similar to what you want to write.

Resources:

- *Draft No. 4: On the Writing Process* – John McPhee

- *Write to Market: Deliver a Book that Sells* – Chris Fox

- K-lytics genre/niche reports: www.TheCreativePenn.com/genre

- KDP Rocket for category and keyword research: www.TheCreativePenn.com/rocket

2.5 Decide on your book title

You don't have to decide on your book title before you've written it. You can use a working title for the project. For example, I've started writing a book on creating from the shadow side and using our inner darkness to bring depth to our writing. But at the moment, I don't know what the final title will be, so I'm just calling it *The Shadow Book*.

That's fine until I understand exactly what I'm writing, and I'll give it a title later.

Of course, if you *can* narrow it down early on, it will make the whole process easier, so here are some things to consider as you work out your title.

Consider Search-Engine Optimization and keywords

Amazon is a search engine for people who want to buy something. They already have their credit card details loaded, they know they want to buy a book. Will it be yours?

Switch your brain to reader mode. You're not the author anymore. You're a reader in the niche, and you're looking for a book. What would you type into the search bar?

The words you type are keywords or keyword phrases and Amazon will auto-populate the search bar dropdown with the most common keywords. For example, if you go to Amazon.com and start typing in 'how to be a t', it will auto-populate (at the time of writing) with:

- How to be a travel writer

- How to be a tudor

- How to be a teacher

- How to be a tour guide

- How to be a translator

These are already interesting topics and book titles in themselves and you can get a lot of ideas by doing this kind of research.

I use this principle for my books for authors. Can you guess what *How to Market a Book* is about? Or *How to Make a Living with your Writing*? These are clear titles based on keywords.

Check out www.amazon.com/charts (20 bestselling and most read books for the week) for other books like this. For example, *The Instant Pot Electric Pressure Cooker Cookbook: Easy Recipes for Fast and Healthy Meals.* This is selling a LOT of copies. Clearly, Instapots have gone crazy and this is the bestselling cookbook in the niche.

There is no clever title. Not even an exciting book cover. The book does what it says on the tin and that's what readers want.

You can research keywords by doing the manual dropdown search, or you can use tools like KDP Rocket that do this work for you: www.TheCreativePenn.com/rocket

Use the principles of copywriting

Non-fiction book titles often use principles of copywriting. They focus on **benefits** and encourage the reader to take action. For good examples, look at magazine headlines: How to do X, Stop doing Y, Overcome Z, Secrets of A.

Classic benefit driven titles include *How to Win Friends and Influence People* by Dale Carnegie, and *What to Expect When You're Expecting* by Heidi Murkoff, where the reader can clearly understand what they are getting in the title.

You can even take this further and include **time-specific benefits**. For example, *The Four Hour Work Week: Escape the 9-5, Live Anywhere and Join the New Rich* by Timothy Ferriss, or *Lean In 15: The Shift Plan. 15 Minute Meals and Workouts to Keep You Lean and Healthy* by Joe Wicks.

Some titles grab attention with an **element of surprise or shock**. For example, *The Subtle Art of Not Giving a F*ck* by Mark Manson, *Thug Kitchen: Eat like you give a F*ck,* or *You Are a Badass: How to Stop Doubting Your Greatness and Start Living an Awesome Life* by Jen Sincero.

Other titles are like the **listicles** shared so much on social media. For example, *The 22 Immutable Laws of Marketing* by Al Ries and Jack Trout, or *The 7 Habits of Highly Effective People* by Stephen R Covey.

Make it clear what the book is about.

For example, *Astrophysics for People in a Hurry* by Neil deGrassse Tyson. This is a great title. A book on astrophysics might not have a huge audience, but by making it clear that it's a short round-up, a way to grasp the topic without having to know everything, it appeals to people who love pop-science. It's in the same vein as blockbusters like *A Brief History of Time* by Stephen Hawking, or *Sapiens: A Brief History of Humankind* by Yuval Noah Harari.

Don't be clever – unless you use an obvious sub-title

Many authors like the idea of using a personal word or a catchy phrase that has meaning for them, but could be misunderstood by readers. One way to mitigate this is to use a clear, targeted sub-title.

For example, *Irresistible* by Adam Alter. This could be a dessert cookbook, a romance novel, or something on how to attract a partner, but with the sub-title it becomes clear. *The Rise of Addictive Technology and the Business of Keeping Us Hooked.* Interestingly, they changed the sub-title for the Kindle edition to *Why we Can't Stop Checking, Scrolling, Clicking and Watching.* Clearly, the branding of the hardcover didn't do so well.

Another example is *Still Stripping After 25 Years* by Eleanor Burns, which is actually about quilting. The cover makes it quite clear that it's not about the sex industry, but the title alone could be confusing!

Seth Godin, marketing guru and non-fiction bestselling author, had to re-title one of his books because there was so much misunderstanding. The original title was *All Marketers Are Liars.* The sub-title made it clearer: *The Power of Telling Authentic Stories in a Low-Trust World.* Seth eventually changed the title to *All Marketers Tell Stories,* although the cover still has the word Liars crossed out.

Attract your target market

When readers are browsing in a genre, your title should make them think, "Yes, I must read that" and click Buy Now immediately. They must be able to see themselves in the book.

Consider *Word by Word: The Secret Life of Dictionaries* by Kory Stamper. The target market is people who love words, but the title is also a callback to *Bird by Bird* by Anne Lamott, a huge bestseller in the writing community. I was immediately attracted to the book, and although it's a clever title with a play on words, it also has a clear sub-title for those who might not get the reference.

I also recently discovered *High Performance Habits: How Extraordinary People Become That Way* by Brendon Burchard. It's clearly aimed at a specific target audience of people who want to become high achievers, or get to the next level. I bought it pretty quickly in both hardback and audiobook formats. A double win!

Testing your book title

Tim Ferriss split-tested his original book title with Google Adwords, and these days, you can also use Facebook Ads or PickFu, a service that creates a poll for testing covers and titles.

Tim's original title was *Drug Dealing for Fun and Profit*. His first business was in health supplements so it was a 'clever' title with an element of shock which fits some of the copywriting principles. But during his testing phase, he found that *The 4-Hour Work Week* got a better result and he also split-tested covers. The book has been out 10 years and continues to hit the bestseller lists and change lives. It's a modern classic, but possibly would not have been if he had kept the original title.

Consider what people want, not what you think they need

When I left my day job to become a full-time author entrepreneur, I realized pretty quickly that the skills of running a business were quite different to the craft of writing books. A successful author needs both.

So as I learned how to run my own business, I also wrote a book to help others on the same journey, *Business for Authors: How to be an Author Entrepreneur.* It continues to sell a small number every month as it contains everything an author needs, including detail on accounting and tax, topics that aren't sexy but critical for business.

I couldn't work out why this book wasn't selling well when it was so clearly needed in the author community and it had great reviews. Then I considered the title and the topics in it, and decided to write a cut-down version containing the highlights in a more easily consumable way without all the technical business stuff. That became *How to Make a Living with your Writing,* which is my bestselling non-fiction book in every format, and was included in a list of the Best Business Books in 2015 by INC magazine.

In another example, Tony Robbins originally published *Money: Master the Game*, a doorstop book packed with interviews and tips and basically way too much information for the average person. Clearly, it didn't hit the market he wanted it to, as he later published *Unshakeable: Your Financial Freedom Playbook*, a cut-down version in a much more easily digestible format that I recommend to anyone interested in investing.

Changing your book title after publication

If you already have your book out and now want to change the title, don't worry, it can be done!

If you have control of your book – either you self-published or got the rights back from your publisher – you can re-publish the book with a new title and a new cover. Just upload a new version of the book, over-writing the previous ebook edition so it retains reviews, but you will need a new ISBN for print editions.

I changed the title of my first book from *How to Enjoy Your Job or Find a New One* to *Career Change* for keyword search reasons. There were 10 times as many searches for 'career change' than for 'how to enjoy your job,' so my sales went up after the change purely through organic search. If you search for 'career change' now on Amazon, my book should still be on page one.

Hopefully this chapter has given you some ideas for shaping your book title, or perhaps coming up with a list of them that you can test with your target market.

Questions:

- What are some of the top-selling titles in your niche? Do they have anything in common?

- What are the types of book titles that attract you as a reader?

- Have you done SEO research on Amazon or using one of the available tools?

- How could you use copywriting tips to improve your title?

- Are you considering what people want as well as what they need?

- What are some possible book titles for your book? How could you test these?

Resources:

- KDP Rocket for category and keyword research: www.TheCreativePenn.com/rocket

- PickFu for book title/cover testing: www.TheCreativePenn.com/pickfubook

2.6 Your author name and pseudonyms

If you're considering a long-term writing career that goes beyond one or two books, your author name will become a brand in a reader's head – a promise of what to expect from your writing, an indication of what experience they will have every time. So your author name is more important than you might think and something to consider before you move forward with book cover design.

What name should you use?

Of course, you can use your real name to publish your books. There is no issue with that for most people, but it's worth checking whether someone else is already using that name on Amazon and whether you can get the domain name for your website.

For example, if your name is Dan Brown, you'll find that author name already taken. Even if you're writing about particle physics, it will still be confusing for readers, so you're better off adding a middle initial or using your middle name.

Another consideration is whether it's **easy to say your name and website out loud** on podcasts/radio interviews/media. Not just for you, but for other people. A distinctive name is great, but if people can't read it or spell it, it will be challenging for people to remember and you'll always be spelling it out. Audio and video are a huge part of marketing now, so this is an important consideration even if you can't see that far into the journey yet.

Consider the market that you're targeting

For example, if you're marketing to readers in the US and UK and you have a name that is hard to pronounce for English speakers, you could consider Anglicizing it. If you're aiming to sell primarily in your own country market, then this will be less of an issue.

I've had this problem with my thriller name, J.F.Penn, because when I say it out loud, the F can sound like an S, so I have to clearly enunciate on interviews. I also usually say 'Penn with a double n.'

Practice saying your name out loud as if you're on an interview and see how it sounds. Do you have to spell it out? Could it be confusing? Can you get the domain name?

The impact of big data and algorithms for discoverability

Your author name is used by the online bookstores to group your books together on author pages, and you can have a different author page per name. Here are my author pages on Amazon:

http://author.to/JoannaPenn

http://author.to/JFPenn

http://author.to/PennyAppleton

My Joanna Penn page clearly classifies me as a non-fiction author, and if you look at the authors listed as similar, they are all non-fiction. Compare that to my pages for J.F.Penn and Penny Appleton, and now imagine what a muddle this would be if I wrote all these types of books under one name.

Essentially, your author name separates your audience into more easily targetable types of readers. The Amazon algorithm recommends books based on data gathered from purchases and views, so that People who Bought X Also Bought Y, linking together books in a similar genre. You want the algorithm to be able to easily identify the readers for your book, as this will help the system sell for you.

Some writers choose to write in multiple genres under the same name, but if you're just starting out, consider the ramifications of increasing big data and algorithmic book discovery over time.

When to consider a pseudonym

A pseudonym or pen-name is a name you write under that is different to your real name. It can be a variation on your real name, or something completely different. There are a number of reasons why you might consider a pseudonym.

To protect privacy. This is especially relevant if you have a professional career that you want to keep completely separate, or if you're writing about a sensitive topic.

To differentiate brands and genres as outlined above. I have Joanna Penn (non-fiction), J.F.Penn (thrillers), Penny Appleton (sweet romance).

To disguise gender, although this is more common in the fiction world, e.g. JK Rowling writing in the male-dominated fantasy genre, Lawrence Block using female pen-names for romance, or George Eliot, whose real name was Mary Ann Evans, writing at a time when women weren't accepted as writers.

If the author's name is hard to remember or is unusual. Ayn Rand of *Atlas Shrugged*, was actually Alisa Zinovyevna Rosenbaum, and Joseph Conrad's real name was Jozef Teodor Konrad Korzeniowski.

When you publish under a pseudonym, you can use a different author name in the specific field on the publishing platforms. There are other fields for legal name and bank account name, so you don't need a separate legal business to write under a different name.

If you register copyright, you can do it with both names. I include my pseudonym and my legal name on the copyright registration form.

[Note: it is not necessary to register your manuscript for copyright to be applied. Your work is your copyright as soon as it is created. See chapter 3.14 for more on legal issues.]

You can interact online and in real life under your pseudonym. In fact, I have several author friends whose 'real' name I know, but I still call them by their pseudonym because that's how I always think of them.

Many authors with pseudonyms keep their identity secret, but of course, it is possible that you will be found out. E.L.James was identified as Erika Leonard after she made a gazillion dollars with *50 Shades of Grey*. But perhaps with that level of success, she doesn't mind!

The pros and cons of writing under multiple author names

I love writing under multiple author names because it clearly separates my promise to the reader with each different type of book. It also helps the algorithms target my book to the appropriate readers.

Plus, it enables me to segment my time. I schedule my time by author name and per project, so I keep the balance of my darker, thriller persona alongside serving my non-fiction audience. This helps me manage both commercial and more artistic projects.

However, it does mean segmenting my audience and marketing efforts, splitting my focus and limited time. I have three websites, three email lists, and multiple social media profiles. I have to balance my writing time, promotional schedule and budget across the three author names.

Would I be more successful at this point if I had just picked one author name and focused on that?

Perhaps.

It's clear that authors who write one type of book under one author name and focus 100% on serving a primary audience with multiple books per year can make a great living from book sales. But one of the key aspects of being a creative entrepreneur for the long-term is to **know yourself**, and I need both fiction and non-fiction in order to be creatively fulfilled and make a good living with my writing. So it all depends on your definition of success, your personality type and what you want to do with your life.

You get to choose.

Questions:

- Have you checked whether your author name is already used on Amazon?

- Can you get the domain name for it?

- If not, what are some other variations you could use e.g. middle name or initials

- Is it easy to say your name out loud on a podcast, video, radio or media interview?

- What are some of the pros and cons of using a pseudonym?

2.7 How long does your book have to be?

"I don't know what length to make it. Would it be better
to write a short book people can get through quickly
or a longer one that goes into more depth? I've bought
books in the past that felt 'padded' because the author had
decided to make them 50,000 words or more despite their
topic not really warranting that much! But I'm wary of
making the book *too* short in case it doesn't seem like
good value for money."

Ali Luke, from The Creative Penn survey

The length of your book will depend on a number of considerations.

(1) Do you want to be traditionally published?

If yes, then most publishers still work on specific word
count lengths for books so you'll probably be aiming for
around 60,000-80,000 words for non-fiction. Book size is
often based on how thick the spine will be and how it will
stand out in a bookstore – although things are changing.
Check the submission guidelines for agents and publishers
you want to pitch.

If you're self-publishing, length means little, as we mainly
do marketing online and sell print-on-demand. The size is
less important than the value to the customer.

(2) What do you want to do with the book?

Is it a magnum opus and the cornerstone of a high-priced speaking event? Is it for kudos / status / authority? Is it a business card? Are you gifting it to clients? Does it need to feel weighty?

If yes, you'll probably be looking at 50,000-80,000 words so it's chunky enough to fit in your hand.

My books *Business for Authors*, *The Healthy Writer* and *How to Market a Book* are all around 70,000 words, and this book is around 60,000.

Is it part of a series of micro-topics? Are you doing digital only? How much are you charging for it?

A book can be 25,000 words and still be of incredible value if it is priced appropriately. For example, check out S.J.Scott's non-fiction books on habits for US$2.99.

How long does it have to be in order to print it?

How to Make a Living with your Writing is my shortest non-fiction book at 27,000 words and looks fine in print. Just be sure to price appropriately.

Don't make it too long. Don't pack it with everything you have to give.

A good example of over-delivering is *Money, Master the Game* by Tony Robbins. I'm an avid reader of investment books, and it was dense even for me. It clearly didn't reach enough people as Tony produced *Unshakeable,* a cut-down version, which is much easier to learn from and put into practice.

Essentially, you don't need to pad your book out to increase the word count. Non-fiction readers, in particular, want value fast. Make it actionable, helpful, and great value and the length won't matter.

Questions:

- If you want a traditional publishing deal, what are the word count specifications in the submission guidelines?

- What do you want to use your book for? How will that shape the length you are aiming for?

- What are some of the books you consider to be 'padded,' and what are the books you found great value regardless of their length?

2.8 How long will it take to write the book?

Many authors want to know how long it will take to write their book. But this question depends on a number of factors.

What kind of book is it?

A magnum opus of 100,000 words will take a lot longer than a self-help book of just 25,000 words.

How much research do you need to do?

How much time do you need to prepare the material before you write the book? Is this a topic you're already immersed in and know about, or do you need to start from scratch?

How experienced a writer are you?

A journalist who has never written a book but is used to writing words to deadline will be a lot faster than someone more used to spending months thinking before writing.

How many words per hour can you write?

This will be an approximate number that you can work out once you have been writing for a while. It's good to get some idea of word count over time.

How many hours can you allocate to write?

The more hours you can commit, the faster you will get the first draft done. There is usually a maximum number of hours you can produce creatively at one time without your brain exploding, so make sure to factor that in. Writing is tiring!

How well-structured is the book? How much editing is needed?

Editing is not about typos and grammatical errors. They can be fixed by a proofreader in the final read-through. But if the structure of the book doesn't work, then the amount of time for rewrites can be considerable, as you will need to re-organize the material to make it work for the reader. The more editing you need, the longer the book will take.

An example of how long it takes

Jane wants to write a book on *How to Run a Successful Food Truck Business*, aimed at chefs who want to take their cooking out to events and markets. She has never written a book before, but she's motivated and wants to help people, as well as create a small income stream that is not reliant on her making food. She spends a dedicated week reading other food truck books and taking notes, then comes up with a table of contents with 18 chapters. She is aiming for a book of around 25,000 words.

Jane spends an hour each weekday writing before her kids get up and before getting into her day job. She works the food truck at the weekend, so she doesn't write then, although she does keep notes of her ideas. She manages 1000 words per writing session, so it takes her 25 writing days, or five weeks, to complete the first draft.

Then she uses that hour to edit the book. It takes her 15 days/ three weeks elapsed time to edit the book to where she is happy. Then she sends it to an editor, who suggests some more improvements, which take her another ten days/two weeks. In total, Jane has a completed manuscript in 10-14 weeks elapsed time. I'd also suggest a proofreader which will add another week or so.

Of course, your situation will be different based on the variables above. There are some authors who can write a book in a weekend, working intensely and using processes like dictation to speed the writing time. Others may take months or even years considering the detail of what they want to write and slowly shaping the book.

Make a plan and schedule your time

In the end, how long your book takes will come down to your life choices and personality as well as how much you really want to get your book into the world.

You need to take control of your writing schedule, or you will end up being one of those writers who start a book and never finish it.

Make a plan and schedule time blocks for your book.

That's how I'm writing this book right now. I booked a two-hour slot at a co-working space near me because I find it easier to create when I'm away from my normal desk.

If I pay for space, I will definitely turn up for the meeting with myself, and two hours is a good block to write without getting too tired. I also write at a local café in the mornings after it opens at 7 am. It doesn't matter where or when you get the writing blocks in, but you need to schedule them. So get out your diary and work out when you can write. Assume you will manage 500 words per hour and schedule as many blocks as you need to get a first draft done.

"Nobody cares much whether you write or not.
You just have to do it."

Natalie Goldberg, Writing Down the Bones

Questions:

- What kind of book are you aiming to write and how will that impact your target length?

- How much research do you need to do?

- How experienced a writer are you?

- How many words per hour can you write?

- How many hours can you allocate for writing?

- How well-structured is the book? How much editing is needed?

- Have you allocated time in your schedule to write your book and worked out how long it might take you?

2.9 Your perspective on time

> "People claim to want to do something that matters, yet they measure themselves against things that don't, and track their progress not in years but in microseconds. They want to make something timeless, but they focus instead on immediate payoffs and instant gratification."

Ryan Holiday, Perennial Seller

Your perspective on time will shape the non-fiction book you write. Compare these two scenarios.

Writer A wants to write a book that will help people and change lives. He also wants to make money quickly, so he writes a short book aimed at a hungry market with a killer title that promises quick wins. The book rises in the charts, he makes some money, and then he moves onto the next project, growing his backlist quickly, preparing for another spike launch.

Writer B wants to write a book that will help people and change lives. She'd love to make some money, but she's not in such a hurry that she rushes the process. She wants to create a book that will sell for years to come. She is focusing on creating a body of work that lasts.

There is room for both of these approaches in publishing.

There always has been. So this is not a value judgment, but more of a question that you must answer for yourself and for each book.

What is your definition of success for this book?

Is the book a short-term money-maker or an important piece of your body of work?

You can, of course, do both. But perhaps not with the same book.

When I look at my non-fiction books, I have examples of both. I wrote *Business for Authors* as a handbook to being a creative entrepreneur. It forms a keystone of my body of work and represents a shift in my thinking.

But it didn't sell many copies, and I wanted to reach people – and yes, make some money – so I wrote a shorter version, *How to Make a Living with your Writing*. That book is my bestselling non-fiction title, but it will eventually be obsolete as the industry changes. I have to keep updating it.

The Successful Author Mindset is the book I get most emails about. The book that writers read again and again because it touches on the self-doubt and fear at the heart of the creative life. It has never been a breakout hit, but it sells consistently well, and more importantly, it changes people's lives and is a crucial part of my creative journey.

So your book can define you, it can be a touchstone on your journey.

Or it can be a short, useful How To book that makes you some cash but isn't something you will think about on your death-bed.

As Elizabeth Gilbert says in *Big Magic*, "You're not required to save the world with your creativity. Your art not only doesn't have to be original, in other words, it also doesn't have to be important."

There's room for both in your life and on the myriad bookshelves of the world, and I hope you will write both over your creative life. I've found that as soon as you clear the creative pipe of one book, another idea appears, or many more ideas and you will soon be writing the next one.

The more books you write, the less one particular book will define you, and perhaps that is the most freeing thing. Because we all change, we all shift perspectives, and each book represents a point on that journey.

Some writers shift more radically than others over time.

Consider Neil Strauss, who wrote *The Game: Penetrating the Secret Society of Pickup Artists* in 2005. He became infamous for dating advice that belittled women, but then in 2015, he wrote *The Truth: An Uncomfortable Book about Relationships*, which focused on finding love and is a "painfully honest account of a life crisis forced upon me by my own behavior."

Write from where you are now and keep writing even as your life changes.

> "Do I contradict myself? Very well, then, I contradict myself. I am large, I contain multitudes."
>
> *Walt Whitman*

Questions:

- What is your definition of success for this book? Is the book a short-term money-maker or an important piece of your body of work?

- What is your perspective on time and what you will create along the author journey?

Resources:

- *Perennial Seller: The Art of Making and Marketing Work that Lasts* – Ryan Holiday

- *Big Magic: Creative Living Beyond Fear* – Elizabeth Gilbert

2.10 Writing a book proposal

"Book proposals force you to consider the
kinds of fundamental questions, both personal and
professional, that alter lives. Writing one helps define
who you are as a writer and how you want to make
your mark upon the world.

It provides a systematic context that encourages
you to focus your work, memorialize your ideas, and
celebrate you. Writing a proposal can be – and often is
– a transformative experience."

Jody Rein & Michael Larsen,
How to Write a Book Proposal, 5th Edition

Book proposals are used in traditional publishing to
outline the business case for a potential book, its audience
and marketing potential. Many non-fiction books start out
as a proposal and publishing contracts are often based on
the proposal even before the book is written.

A proposal is not necessary for independent authors
because you decide what to write and publish, but it is a
useful tool however you choose to publish. It focuses your
mind on what you're trying to achieve and helps you consider aspects beyond the writing.

Here are some sections to consider in your proposal.

Analysis of comparison titles (known as 'comps')

By now, you should know the 5-10 books that are similar to yours. Outline the sub-categories they sell in, include title and keyword analysis, and consider what sets your book apart from the others.

Target audience

Chapter 2.3 goes into how to identify your target market, but for a proposal, you should take it further, preferably citing authoritative sources in your genre.

Consider the desire for the book. How will your book fulfill a need in your target market? What are the benefits to the reader? Why is it worth publishing?

Author bio

Your background and why you are the right person to write this book, as well as your credentials if relevant. If you have previously published, then sales figures and awards might be appropriate here.

Your author platform and marketing plan

Publishers want to know that the book will sell, and your ability to reach people will play a huge part in whether they decide to publish the book. This is why so many non-fiction authors start out with a popular blog, podcast, YouTube channel, speaking career, public-facing job/business, journalism career or another way of reaching an audience.

You should cite verifiable numbers here (if they are worth listing), e.g. email list subscribers, blog traffic, podcast downloads, social media follows, speaking engagements or any other evidence of your ability to reach an existing market that is relevant for your book.

Remember to consider your network and existing relationships that might expand your marketing reach. List quotes or endorsements from other bestselling authors/ public figures, or evidence that you can reach out to other authors/bloggers/podcasters for help.

Overview of the book

A paragraph outlining the book that draws the reader in and makes them want more. Easier said than done!

Table of contents/chapter outline

This can be a list, or you could go into more detail and flesh out the chapters with a few lines each.

Sample chapter/s

Include evidence of your ability to write if you are pitching a publisher. Don't use an introduction, but rather something that gives a flavor of the work and your writing style.

Submitting your proposal to a publisher

Some authors will get obsessed with how many pages a proposal is meant to be, or what font it should be typed in. These things are minor compared to clearly articulating your author platform, the benefit to the reader, and targeting your proposal to the right publisher.

Questions:

- Are you submitting to an agent or traditional publisher? Have you looked at their guidelines around book proposals or researched examples of proposals that have sold in your niche?

- However you aim to publish, have you considered the aspects outlined for a book proposal?

Resources:

- *How to Write a Book Proposal, 5th Edition* – Jody Rein & Michael Larsen

- Round-up of resources on book proposals from Jane Friedman: www.JaneFriedman.com/start-here-how-to-write-a-book-proposal

Part 3: Writing and Editing

3.1 Gather and organize existing material

"I am a story-teller, and I look to academic research …
for ways of augmenting story-telling."

Malcolm Gladwell

Many non-fiction writers already have a lot of material they have generated over the years. If you gather up what you already have, the bulk of the book may be there already. Here are some possible things you might have:

- Recordings of talks/workshops that you can get transcribed

- Blog posts

- Articles written for magazines/media

- PowerPoint or Keynote decks of slides

- Workbooks

- Handouts or papers from events

- Training material

- Journals/notebooks

- Evernote folders full of articles

- Survey questions from your audience

- Blog or YouTube video comments

- Feedback forms from events

- Notes from books or Kindle Highlights you
can export

This can be overwhelming, especially if you have a lot of material, but you can find rich seams of information and personal stories if you have a look through what you already have.

Digging through the past

I use excerpts from my journals in *Career Change, The Successful Author Mindset* and *The Healthy Writer*, snippets from my life when I poured my heart out onto the page. Sharing these in the books brought the words alive and let the reader to hear my authentic voice.

But I have a lot of journals, so it was hard to find those moments in years' worth of writing. I allocated a block of time and paged through the journals, marking useful pages. I remembered a poem I'd written years ago about my migraines, so I hunted for that specifically.

I finally found it in a folder in a box of stuff I hadn't opened for over four years, but it was worth digging out because those lines of pure pain helped me remember what life used to be like. Sharing a transformation can be powerful, so spend some time digging out evidence of your previous self to bring your story alive.

If you do wade through your existing information, consider using a Dictaphone or some kind of recording device to take notes as you go, so you can cull what you need without being drowned in too much information.

Of course, you could just ignore everything and start again with what's in your brain, so don't feel you have to do this.

If you are overwhelmed by it all, go back to basics. Pick one chapter and focus on that. Revisit the reason why you're writing. Take a break, go for a walk and then return to the material with fresh energy. It is a messy process, but that is part of the challenge and the joy, so dive in.

Organizing material

You can use a drive on your computer and copy and paste files into that, or use Evernote or other research apps. I'm a huge fan of Scrivener for organizing material. I start a new Project when I have an idea for a book and throw everything in there: one-liners of ideas or quotes, links to articles, blog posts and more. Once I'm ready to focus on the book, I use that material to shape the table of contents and start to fill in the rest.

"A notetaker becomes a writer when his or her need to write is sustained by a subject that allows, in fact demands, that this be organised into a project."

André Gorz, Letter to D

Questions:

- What existing material do you have already that could be used in the writing process?

- How will you keep everything organized?

Resources:

- Scrivener software for organizing research, planning, writing and formatting: www.LiteratureAndLatte.com

- Evernote app for organization: www.Evernote.com

3.2 Research, interviews, surveys and social listening

"Writing non-fiction is more like sculpture, a matter of shaping the research into the finished thing."

Joan Didion

You don't have to write a book based on just your own knowledge and experience. In fact, that's probably the worst thing to do, as you will likely miss a great deal. Here are some ways to add value to your book.

Read books and take notes

As Pulitzer Prize-winning author, Cormac McCarthy, said, "Books are made out of books." Writers are readers, or these days, maybe audiobook listeners! Reading books by other authors on the same or tangential topics will help you add to your material, prompting other ideas and giving you new directions. Originality and creativity are not often found in brand new ideas, but more in your personal take on a topic.

Some authors worry that they may inadvertently plagiarize other authors. My tip here is to make sure you never copy and paste whole segments from books into your notes. Instead, paraphrase as you go, or if you are going to quote directly, use speech marks in your notebook as well.

Ryan Holiday, author of *Perennial Seller*, uses index cards to take notes on the books he reads, and over time, gathers blocks of these cards which he uses to shape his books, as he described in this interview on The Creative Penn Podcast.

"When I read a book, I usually have a pen, or I fold and mark the things that I think were important. Then, a couple of weeks later, I go back through the book, I take notes, and transfer those to notecards ... then those notecards are organized by theme in boxes, and each book is normally its own box. That's my personal system."

Interviews with experts

"My rule is that if I interview someone, they should never read what I have to say about them and regret having given me the interview."

Malcolm Gladwell

You don't have to be the expert if you collate interviews with experts and present the material in a coherent way. You can also bring a whole new level of depth to a book if you include excerpts from interviews or tips from people who have achieved the transformation presented in the book.

Steven Pressfield talked about doing this in an interview on The Creative Penn Podcast for *The Lion's Gate*, where he spent months in Israel interviewing veterans from the Six Day War.

"The history was still there. So I went over to Israel, and I interviewed 67 or something veterans, fighter pilots, tankers, men and women, and I had 400 hours of interviews."

You can also include the interviews in a podcast or series of audio or video extras that go with the book. This can be extra marketing, bonus content, or the basis of a multimedia course.

Surveys

If you have an audience already, then doing a survey can be an incredibly powerful way to find out the problems and questions that your market has.

I surveyed my audience for *The Healthy Writer* and the experiences of those who responded shaped the table of contents. We included quotes throughout the book from writers going through various health issues. I also did a survey for this book in order to understand the questions and concerns of writers and subsequently added new chapters I would have missed on my own.

If you do an original survey, you can use the results in marketing material. Traditional media is always interested in a survey that demonstrates something interesting, so consider how you could word your questions in a way that will make the information useful later.

I use free Google Forms for surveys, but you can also use a premium site like SurveyMonkey, which has more extended functionality.

Consent and permission

With surveys and interviews, be sure to include a section about consent to use the gathered material in your book and/or for marketing purposes. You could also use snippets under the terms of fair use, as covered in chapter 3.14 on legal issues.

Social listening

You can find out what questions people have about topics by looking at hashtags on Twitter or Instagram, joining groups on Facebook, checking out sites like Quora, or looking at Google Trends or what is trending on YouTube around your niche. People are always asking questions and responding to ideas in public, so you can get ideas as well as looking at the language they use by doing this kind of social listening.

You have to stop sometime!

All these ideas can be fantastic for generating more material, but beware of analysis paralysis. You can do just-in-time research as you write, as well as starting from scratch and filling parts in later. You might be surprised by how much is actually in your brain. You know more than you think.

So revisit your writing schedule, use the time you've allocated for research but don't get lost in the weeds. Make sure you stop researching and start writing!

Questions:

- How can you expand on your research with these methods?

- Have you asked for all the appropriate permissions and consent for using the information in your book?

- How can you prevent yourself from being lost in analysis paralysis?

Resources:

- Interview with Ryan Holiday on his non-fiction process: www.TheCreativePenn.com/ryan1

- Interview with Steven Pressfield on his research process for *The Lion's Gate*, mental toughness and Resistance: www.TheCreativePenn.com/pressfield1

- Google Forms: docs.google.com/forms

- Survey Monkey: www.SurveyMonkey.com

3.3 Structure and organize the book

"Non-fiction requires enormous discipline. You construct
the terms of your story, and then you stick to them."

Barbara Kingsolver

Although non-fiction books don't contain the classic narrative arc of novels, they still need to take the reader on a
journey of understanding. You can't jump around as you'll
end up confusing the reader and that is the cardinal sin.
As thriller author, Jeffrey Deaver once said, "The reader is
god." You need to please the reader if you want more sales,
more reviews and more lives changed.

I've often found that the structure of my non-fiction
books only falls into place once I have written quite a few
chapters. I'll have lots of placeholders that disappear, are
absorbed into other chapters or expanded into new sections. So, don't worry if you're struggling with structure.
You don't need to nail it up front, just be aware of it, and
keep iterating as you write.

Think in Parts or Sections first

These broad categories will help you fill in the blanks later.
For this book, it was obvious that I needed a section on
Before you Write, then one on the actual writing, then
publishing and then marketing. That is a clear linear pro-
gression for this book and your journey as an author.

For *The Healthy Writer*, we struggled on the order of the chapters until late in the writing process when it became clear that the transformation was from Unhealthy to Healthy Writer. We structured the book into those two main parts, and then everything fell into place.

Outline your draft Table of Contents

Now you have your specific topic and a lot of research notes, it's time to start outlining your table of contents. You've gone wide with a lot of ideas, but now you need to bring the content back to what will be relevant for this particular book.

You'll likely cut a lot of your material out, and some of your ideas might even end up in another book. When I wrote *Business for Authors: How to be an Author Entrepreneur,* I had a whole load of ideas on the psychology of writing. But that section ended up growing so big that I carved those chapters out and they became the seed of *The Successful Author Mindset.*

Whenever I get an idea for a book, I create a new Scrivener project and use the Binder area to add ideas for chapters. These are often just one-liners when I start out, but then I hone the Table of Contents from those initial thoughts. Scrivener enables you to drag and drop chapters, which makes re-ordering them super-easy.

Of course, you can use MS Word, Google Docs, another word processing program, or spreadsheets. Whatever works for you.

You could also use mind mapping, a visual way of organizing information. Start by writing the main topic in the middle of the page and then brainstorm outwards, creating hierarchical branching trees that go deeper into each sub-topic. There are lots of different software options for mind mapping, but you can also just use pen and paper to get the ideas flowing.

If you prefer to talk through your ideas, try dictation, covered in more detail in chapter 3.5. Or you could ask someone to interview you on your chosen topic, and use the transcript as the basis for your Table of Contents.

However you choose to work, you'll need to come up with a coherent list of chapters. You can change the order later, so at this stage, just make a list of all the different topics under your sections.

Use sub-headings

If you want to take your organization a step further, you can use sub-headings within each chapter to split the material into easily digestible chunks. Many non-fiction readers skim through books, looking for the most pertinent and useful sections, and sub-headings help the reader find what they're looking for.

Other sections to consider

At this stage, you can use placeholder headings to collect other material and ideas. This can be firmed up later as you work through the book, but it's a good idea to make sure you collect it all along the way.

You might want to include **extras** like case studies, check-lists, exercises, downloadable audio or workbook pages, images, illustrations and other extras. These can be self-contained in the book or you can include links back to your website for multi-media.

Resources, bibliography and references. Keep a list as you go so it's not a nightmare to collect at the end. Trust me, I know all about that!

Foreword and blurb quotes

You certainly don't need a foreword. But if you do want one and have someone in mind, then make sure you ask them well in advance. The same goes for blurb quotes. Just ask in advance and keep a note of people to contact later.

Acknowledgments

This is where the author credits the people who helped bring the book into being, so keep a list of people you work with along the way so you can pull it together later.

Author bio

Your credentials and experience, or whatever makes you interesting.

Email list sign-up

You want to be able to capture people's email addresses so you can contact them later for marketing reasons, or when you have a new book. Consider what you will offer at the end of the book to entice them to sign up, or whether you have something extra as part of the book e.g. download-able audio.

By now, you should have a list of chapters that you need to fill in.

Questions:

- How will you structure your book? What are the top-level parts and how can you break those down to lead the reader through a journey?

- What are the extra sections that you might consider as you write?

Resources:

- Scrivener software for organizing research, planning, writing and formatting: www.LiteratureAndLatte.com

3.4 How to write the first draft

"Almost all good writing begins with terrible first efforts.
You need to start somewhere."

Anne Lamott, Bird by Bird

When you haven't written a book before, you assume it's easy enough to do, until you try it! I still find first drafts challenging after 27+ books, but I have some specific processes and tools that help me get it done.

Schedule time blocks for writing – and ONLY write in that time

Scheduling writing time is the secret weapon because if you get your butt in the chair, or stand and dictate, for consistent periods of time, you WILL finish a draft.

Get out your calendar and schedule time for writing, as you would for any other important commitment. Then turn up for that meeting with yourself, and write. It doesn't matter if the words aren't very good. You can clean them up in the editing process, but you need to get black on white and finish that first draft in order to edit it into something useful later.

Don't do anything else in that time block. No email, no social media, no Slack or messaging. Just get words on the page.

Find a location that will help you create

Our brains get used to specific locations for specific things. If you always watch TV from the couch, you'll sit down on it and automatically turn the TV on. If you use the home office for email or accounts, or if it's cluttered with children's projects, or unfinished DIY or artwork, you'll find it hard to write in there.

I write most of my first drafts in a local café these days. I get there when it opens at 7 am and write until 9.30-10 am, when I go and exercise. I wear noise-cancelling headphones and listen to rain and thunderstorms on repeat. I drink one black coffee per hour, leaving when it starts to get busy so they can use the table for higher-paying customers.

If I'm dictating a draft, I book a room in a local co-working space and create there. Both of these options cost some money, but the act of getting out of the house and committing to a different location can make all the difference in getting you to write.

Of course, you could use a library or an office space at work if you go in early. I used to write in the London Library when we lived there, and when I had a day job in Australia, I would write from 5 am in the spare room in our house. It was the only way I could fit creative time in before my brain was taken over by the job. The point is to find somewhere you can focus on your book.

Once you are in the location at the specified time, make sure you won't be disturbed. Turn your phone to Do Not Disturb or airplane mode. Turn off social media and email. You can even use an app like Freedom to block your Internet access for a limited time. If you're working from home, put a sign on your door that you should only be disturbed for emergencies. And if you are still disrupted, then get out of the house!

Use timed writing sessions

Pretty much all productivity books talk about the importance of focused work followed by breaks. Timed writing sessions are the best way to chunk it down. Some authors like to use the Pomodoro Technique – 25 minutes writing, 5 minutes break – then repeat several times per session.

Setting a timer can help you focus more intensely on the writing period, then make sure you take a short break. You'll achieve more than if you try and write for an hour or two with no scheduled breaks, especially if you haven't yet acquired the stamina for long writing sessions.

When the timer starts, don't wait for inspiration. The muse doesn't arrive when you sit around wishing it would. It turns up when you start creating, so get writing.

It helps if you have completed your table of contents, as you'll have a list of chapters to fill in. If you haven't done that yet, then use your first writing block to get that done.

Write in any order

Don't try to write the Introduction first. It's often one of the last things to write. It's fine to jump around and write in any order. You might get ideas for other chapters as you focus on a different one, so write down those thoughts and carry on. You can always re-order later.

Track your progress

A book can be a daunting prospect, especially if you feel like the words are hard to produce and you haven't managed much in a particular session. But writing a book is just a series of sentences gathered together into chapters collected into book form. So, if you have managed a sentence, you have taken a step on the journey.

Tracking your progress can help to make you feel like you're achieving. Some authors use spreadsheets to track time writing and number of words. You can also just write them on a wall chart, or in an app.

Scrivener has a Project Targets section where you can set and track word count per session. I also use colored flags, turning the chapters yellow when I have finished the first draft. I turn them blue after editing and green when they are finished and ready to publish. This makes a huge book more visually manageable, and if I can turn one flag yellow by the end of a session, I feel like I have won the day.

When is a first draft finished?

My definition of a first draft is a version of your book that can be read end to end and stands as a coherent whole. It doesn't have "fill this in later," or "write other section here," in it. Yes, it will be rough, and it will need editing, but to get to a finished book, you need a first draft to work on.

Your finished book can be equated to Michelangelo's David, a perfect statue that emerged from a rough block of marble. But first you have to create that block of marble, and for authors, that's the first draft.

How much do you want this?

If you're struggling to find the time to write, then revisit the reason why you're writing in the first place. Does it *really* mean that much to you? Because we all make time for the things we value. If you're not making time for writing, then you don't truly value it.

"The routine produces ... And the routine of doing this six days a week puts a little drop in the bucket each day, and that's the key. Because if you put a drop in a bucket every day, after 365 days, the bucket's going to have some water in it."

John McPhee, Draft No. 4

Questions:

- Have you scheduled time blocks for writing in your calendar? (Not just in your head, but have you actually written them down?)

- Have you found a location where you can write without being disturbed?

- Have you found ways to stop yourself being distracted when you write?

- Are you going to use timed writing sessions? How will you break these up?

- How will you track your progress through the book?

- How will you know when the first draft is finished?

- How much do you want this? What will you say to yourself if you are struggling with writing?

Resources:

- Google Calendar for scheduling time blocks: www.google.com/calendar

- BOSE noise-cancelling headphones. Pricey but worth it. I wear them every time I write now, even when dictating. My link: www.TheCreativePenn.com/silence

- Freedom app: www.freedom.to

- Scrivener software for organizing research, planning, writing and formatting: www.LiteratureAndLatte.com

3.5 How to dictate your book

The word 'writing' has become associated with hitting keys on a keyboard to make letters appear on a screen or inscribing by hand onto paper. But the end result is a mode of communication from one brain to another through the medium of words. Those words can be generated by your voice, just as people can 'read' by listening to an audiobook, an increasingly popular choice for non-fiction.

Famous authors who have written with dictation include diverse creatives John Milton (*Paradise Lost*), Dan Brown, Henry James, Barbara Cartland and Winston Churchill. When Terry Pratchett, fantasy author of the Discworld series, developed Alzheimer's disease, he couldn't write anymore, so he moved to dictation in his final years.

Clearly, dictation is a method that can work for many writers, and it has become an emerging trend for authors these days as technology makes it easier and faster. Why might you consider dictation?

Writing speed and stamina

Dictation is faster at getting words on the page than typing, especially if you're not self-censoring. I've made it up to around 5000 words per hour with dictation, while I only manage about 1500 words per hour by typing.

There is a trade-off with 'finished' words as you will have to do a light edit to correct transcription issues, but if you want to get that first draft done faster, dictation can be the most effective way.

Increased creativity

Some writers have a problem with perfectionism and critical voice in the first draft. They struggle to finish a book because they are constantly editing what they write. If you dictate, you can bypass this critical voice, get the first draft done and then edit it later.

Health reasons

You can dictate standing up or while walking, or lying in bed with injuries, or if pain stops you typing. I started using dictation when I developed RSI, and used it to write the first drafts of my thrillers, *Destroyer of Worlds* and *Map of Shadows*, plus some chapters for *The Healthy Writer*, which I dictated while walking along the canal towpath.

Dictation can help alleviate or prevent pain now, but learning how to write with dictation can also future-proof your living as a writer in case of health problems later.

What's stopping you dictating?

There are a number of reasons why people resist dictation. I know them all because I've been through this journey several times!

The most common are:

- "I'm used to typing. I don't have the right kind of brain for dictation."

- "I don't want to say the punctuation out loud. It will disrupt my flow."

- "I write in public so I can't dictate."

- "I have a difficult accent which will make it impossible."

- "I write fantasy books with weird names which won't work."

- "I don't know how to set it up technically."

- "I can't spare the time to learn how to dictate."

Here's what I wrote in my journal on the first day I tried dictation before I'd even started.

"I'm very self-conscious. I'm worried that I won't be able to find the words. I'm so used to typing and creating through my fingers that doing it with my voice feels strange.

But I learned to type with my fingers, so why can't I learn to type with my words? I just have to practice. Something will shift in my mind at some point, and it will just work.

This should make me a healthier author, and also someone who writes faster. Authors who use dictation are writing incredibly fast. That's what I want. I want to write stories faster as I have so many in my mind that I want to get into the world."

Here are thoughts from my journal *after* the first session:

"It felt like the words were really bad and the story clunky and poor. But actually, when the transcription was done and I edited it, it wasn't as bad as I thought it would be. A classic case of critical voice. I need to ignore this when I'm dictating. I definitely need to plan more before I speak, which will save time overall in both dictation and editing.

I thought I would find the punctuation difficult, but it has also been easier than expected. There are only a few commands that you use regularly, and dialogue is the worst but you get into a rhythm with that. It also gives you a pause between each speaker to consider what they might say next, so perhaps it is a blessing in disguise."

Different methods of dictation

There are two main methods of dictation:

(1) Voice to text in real-time

Use a microphone to dictate straight into a text program, and adjust the words on the screen as you go. You may also be using voice commands to do other tasks e.g. open email, send messages, and more.

(2) Dictate now, transcribe later

Use a recording device to record your words now and later have them transcribed. You can send them to a transcription service like Speechpad.com or you can upload them into Dragon Dictate or another program.

I tried real-time speech-to-text and struggled as watching the words appear on the screen kept my critical voice in the foreground. I wasn't able to speed up as I was always concerned with fixing the errors on-screen.

Now I record directly into my Sony device and later on, I upload into Dragon Dictate on my Mac which creates a .txt file. I copy and paste that into Scrivener and lightly edit the file for the first draft. It's usually pretty exact and this is definitely my preferred process now.

Technical set-up

Speech-to-text technology is improving incredibly fast and will only continue to improve with the mainstream adoption of voice-activated, in-home devices and assistants. There are different apps and hardware and software options, so you don't need everything listed below.

Get started with one variation based on the process you want to use and change as you find out what works for you.

Recording device:

Your options will depend on how you want to dictate and your budget.

- Use your smartphone to record memos through an app like Voice Memos, Evernote or any recording app. There is also a smartphone Dragon Dictation app which syncs with the cloud.

- Hand-held MP3 recorder. I have the Sony ICD-PX333.

- Record straight into your computer/laptop using software like Dragon.

Microphone:

- Desktop microphone to use when recording straight into your computer. I use the Blue Yeti at the moment, but I have used the ATR2100 as well.

- Lavalier microphone / lapel mic for standing/walking which you can plug into your MP3 recorder or smartphone.

- I just talk straight into my hand-held MP3 recorder and it works well enough. You could also talk straight into your smartphone.

The quality of your microphone will make a huge difference to the accuracy of your transcription, so if you are having a lot of errors, look at improving/upgrading your microphone first.

Method for transforming speech-to-text:

- Use a transcription service like Speechpad or find a transcriptionist yourself if you prefer the human touch.

- Many authors use Nuance Dragon which has PC and Mac versions and is the most developed speech-to-text software around.

- Use free built-in software on your computer. On a Mac, use Edit -> Start Dictation. On a PC, use Speech Recognition. Most smart phones have a dictation function for taking notes, or you can use Evernote or other apps.

Tips for getting started with dictation from writers who use it

"The biggest advice that I would give for you and for other writers to get started with dictation is don't try to write that way. The best way to start is to do notes or brainstorming. Take your recorder and just go for a walk. It's almost like free association."

Kevin J. Anderson. International bestselling, award-winning fantasy author who dictates all his books.

"Dragon thinks very differently than we do. So we think in words, right? But Dragon thinks in phrases. So think about what you're going to say and then speak it with confidence. This makes the punctuation easier too."

Monica Leonelle, author of Dictate your Book.

"Embrace dictation as a productivity tool. It's a weapon in your writing arsenal and your workflow. Don't treat it like it's something completely alien.

We're familiar with the keyboard, but that isn't necessarily the best input method anyway. Input methods keep changing. We've had the quill, and then we had the pen and then we had the typewriter and now we have the computer keyboard. In the last few years, we've had touch.

I genuinely believe that the next big input method is voice. In the next 10 years, if you're not embracing voice, you will be behind in the same way as if you don't have a smartphone right now, you're missing out on a lot of technological help."

Scott Baker, author of *The Writer's Guide to Training Your Dragon.*

Questions:

- Why might you consider dictation? How might it help your writing?

- What's stopping you from dictating? How can you work through those issues in order to try it?

- What method of dictation might work for you?

- What tools do you need to get started?

Resources:

- Nuance Dragon speech-to-text software: www.TheCreativePenn.com/dragonsoftware

- Blue Yeti microphone: www.TheCreativePenn.com/blueyeti

- Hand-held MP3 recorder. Sony ICD-PX333: www.TheCreativePenn.com/sony

- *Dictate your Book* – Monica Leonelle

- *The Writer's Guide to Training your Dragon* – Scott Baker

- *Foolproof Dictation* – Christopher Downing

- Interview with Monica Leonelle on *How to Dictate your Book*: www.TheCreativePenn.com/monicadictate

- Interview with Scott Baker on *How to Use Dictation to Write Faster and Stay Healthy*: www.TheCreativePenn.com/scott

3.6 Turn your blog/podcast/ videos into a book

"Not only does blogging offer one of the quickest and easiest ways to write a book, blogging technology allows aspiring authors to promote themselves and their books as they write. This means writers build a following of readers as they blog their books into existence – a following of readers who also will buy a printed book based on those very same blog posts."

Nina Amir, How to Blog a Book

Many non-fiction authors start out with a blog, podcast or YouTube channel before they decide to write a book. They might have reams of content they can use as chapters or at least the basis for chapters in a book.

This worked well for Tim Ferriss, who turned some high-traffic blog posts into the core of *The 4-Hour Body*. He tested chapters on the blog and used the ones that resonated the most in his book.

The idea for *The Successful Author Mindset* came from a blog post on the rollercoaster of being a writer which I then expanded into a book, so this route is certainly possible. But it's not just a copy and paste exercise, as blogging is a different form of writing to the journey through a book. Here are some considerations if you want to turn your blog into a book.

Decide on your angle and create a content plan

You're likely to be blogging in a niche, so you'll have your top-level topic, but you still need to decide on the specific angle for your book and nail down your target market, as per the earlier chapters.

Go through your blog and mine it for useful chapter titles, which will give you some of the content. You will likely find that you need to create more content or adjust what you have to fit your refined topic.

Rewrite and edit the chapters into a coherent journey for the reader

Don't just copy and paste your blog posts into a Word document and then give it to an editor. You need to go through and link the content in a more coherent way. A book has to be a journey for the reader, so you need to lead them through your material. A reader will expect a deeper experience in a book than from skimming a blog post, so your chapters will need to be more considered.

This is the main reason I think blog to book projects are often flawed. Unless they are well-edited, they can just read like a series of episodes without a coherent spine.

From book to blog

While I have used blog posts as the basis for chapters in my books, I generally prefer to go the other way. I use chapters from my books as evergreen articles and videos on my blog. These become shareable content marketing, driving traffic to my site, where people can read excerpts and (hopefully) end up buying my books and courses or signing up for my email list.

"Understand that a non-fiction book is a souvenir, just a vessel for the ideas themselves. You don't want the ideas to get stuck in the book … you want them to spread. Which means that you shouldn't hoard the idea! The more you give away, the better you will do."

Seth Godin

Questions:

- Do you want to turn your blog into a book?

- How can you create a coherent journey through the material and differentiate it from the blog version?

- If you want to go the other way, from book to blog, how can you incorporate chapters in a way that will make them more shareable and bring the text alive?

Resources:

- Example of evergreen article and video based on a chapter from The Successful Author Mindset: www.TheCreativePenn.com/how-do-you-find-the-time-to-write

- *How to Blog a Book: Write, Publish, and Promote Your Work One Post at a Time* – Nina Amir

3.7 Speed, quality and perfectionism

"Perfectionism is self-destructive simply because there's no such thing as perfect. Perfection is an unattainable goal."

Brené Brown, The Gifts of Imperfection

There's a pervasive myth in the writing community that suggests a negative correlation between speed and quality. That a book written quickly is no good. That one written slowly is better than one written fast. That perfection takes years.

This belief can stop you from writing. It can be a block.

Speed and quality

Speed of creation does have a relationship to book length, as it will likely take longer to write a 500,000 word magnum opus on *The History of America* than it will to write a 25,000 word ebook on *How to Cook Easy Gluten-Free Dinners for Kids in 15 Minutes*. These books serve different purposes, and the authors will have quite different definitions of success in mind.

The idea of 'quality' is therefore related to two different elements – what the author thinks, and what the reader thinks about the book.

It is up to you, the author, to create a product that fits your definition of quality, however you choose to publish. After all, plenty of pointless celebrities have book deals with traditional publishers, so the publishing method is hardly a measure of quality. You have to be satisfied that you have done the very best job you can do on this book, and achieved your definition of success.

If you care about critics, then for sure, you want to consider them. But for most non-fiction authors, the main measure of quality is satisfying readers and having reviews that reflect this. If *How to Cook Easy Gluten-Free Dinners for Kids in 15 Minutes* provides value for busy mums trying to give their kids healthier food, and it gets great reviews, then it is a quality book. No matter if it only took two weeks to write.

Authors tend to criticize books far more than readers do, so keep focused on helping your readers and doing the best you can for them.

Perfectionism

Of course, you can only reach readers if you put the book into the world. Some writers find it hard to press 'Publish' because they struggle with letting the book go. They keep messing with sentences, searching in vain for the right turn of phrase. They agonize for weeks, changing back and forth, and finally settle on a sentence, then move onto the next one, only to come back weeks later and begin more revisions.

The truth is that nothing is ever perfect and it's only your fear holding you back.

Even if you hire three separate editors and use ten different proofreaders, you will still get an email from a reader pointing out a typo or an error. This is normal. Go pick up any bestselling book from a traditional publisher and scour it for typos. You will find them.

Look at any prize-winning or bestselling book on Amazon and check the reviews. The more popular the book, the more issues people will find with it. There will never be a book that will satisfy everyone, and that's fine. Not everyone will like your book, and a couple of typos are not the end of the world.

Strive for excellence and follow a professional process to ensure your book is the best it can be

Go through your own self-editing process, then work with a professional editor, do the rewrites that will improve your book and use a proofreader. But make sure you set a deadline, otherwise this editing process can turn into procrastination.

Once you have been through a rigorous process with an end point, get your book out into the world, however you choose to publish. If you feel the itch to edit yet again, be honest with yourself.

Is another round of changes really going to make a substantial difference to this book?

Would it be better to work on the next book instead of constantly reworking this one? Do you want to be one of those authors who has been working on the same book for ten years with no end in sight?

At some point, you have to stop listening to your inner critic or the negative voices of others. Do your best and let the book out into the world.

> "Set a limit on revisions, set a limit on drafts, set a time limit … The book will never be perfect."
>
> *Kristine Kathryn Rusch, The Pursuit of Perfection and How it Harms Writers*

Questions:

- What are your thoughts on the relationship between speed and quality?

- How will you define quality for your book and how will you make sure you achieve that without falling into the perfectionism trap?

Resources:

- *The Pursuit of Perfection and How it Harms Writers* – Kristine Kathryn Rusch

- Article on writing fast and its relationship to quality by prolific author, Dean Wesley Smith – www.DeanWesleySmith.com/killing-the-sacred-cows-of-publishing-writing-fast

3.8 Focus and shiny object syndrome

"The road to hell is paved with works-in-progress."

Philip Roth

Writing is simple, but it's not easy.

There will always be distractions, and finishing a project has a lot to do with your ability to focus over a period of time and avoid shiny object syndrome.

What is shiny object syndrome?

"Ooh look, a new idea! That is so cool, much more interesting than this old idea I'm working on over here. Why don't I just spend a bit of time on that new, shiny project and leave the old one in the corner. I'll go back to it later."

You have no doubt felt this urge before, and if you give into it every time, you will never finish the project in hand. Of course, it's a wonderful thing to have new ideas all the time, but if you keep indulging them, they can also be a form of procrastination and resistance.

So when you're in the middle of an existing project, and you're struck by a new shiny idea, acknowledge it, write it down in just a couple of sentences, then turn back to your work in progress.

Finding focus

Don't try to work on more than one project at a time, especially if you're starting out. Focus is the act of concentrating your activity and energy into one thing, and it's critical if you want to finish your book. We all have limited time, and if you're splitting your focus, you will struggle.

Revisit the first principles. Schedule a block of time. It doesn't have to be hours, just 15 minutes is fine if that's all you can spare. Set a timer and write on your book project, or edit, or do whatever is needed to move it forward. Stop when the timer goes off.

You will have taken a step toward your goal. It might be a small step, but there will be some sentences that will make it to your final book, and if you repeat that process, you *will* finish.

Many writers fail because they feel like they need huge blocks of time for their book, but most working writers get black on white in the spaces between the rest of life.

"You must finish what you start."

Robert A. Heinlein, from Heinlein's Rules

Questions:

- Do you suffer from shiny object syndrome? Do you have lots of unfinished projects on the go?

- How will you structure your time so you finish this book? How will you keep yourself on track?

3.9 Writer's block

"The word block suggests that you are constipated or stuck, when the truth is that you're empty."

Anne Lamott, Bird by Bird

Most writers have struggled with getting words on the page at some point. But writer's block is not a monolithic disease with one cause and one cure. The term is often used as a catch-all for a number of issues which have different causes and solutions.

Some of the blocks are caused by fears, anxieties and mindset issues, as covered in chapter 1.5, but here are some more examples of when you might find writing grinding to a halt.

You're a new writer working on your first book

The 'block' at this point is often not knowing *how* to write a book, so you end up flailing around and wasting time, frustrated because you're not getting anywhere. It might be due to lack of ideas or how to string them together, but more often it's just a lack of knowledge on the process. Hopefully, this book will help you with that.

You might also have a block around the kind of book you intend to write. Perhaps you think you need to write a Pulitzer Prize-winning tome that will take years to complete, but the thought of something so massive paralyzes you.

Don't worry. You don't need to write an 'important' book that becomes a classic and stands the test of time. Pick something simple, shorter, and less ambitious to start with. You can always work up to that magnum opus later.

What do you love to read? What do you choose as a guilty pleasure in a bookstore? Be honest with yourself, even if you come from a literary background. What's fun for you? Then go write that.

"I had assembled enough material to fill a silo, and now I had no idea what to do with it … If I was blocked by fear, I was also stymied by inexperience."

John McPhee, Draft No. 4

You're stuck in the 'saggy middle'

A block in the middle of a book can be due to a lack of research and knowledge, or perhaps you need more time to synthesize your ideas on the topic so you can write about it.

Take a break and fill your creative well. Think of your mind as a pipe. You have to put things in the top for ideas to come out the bottom, transformed. Set aside some time to take another look at other books on the subject. What might you have missed?

Another reason for a block here is that you think your book is too short and you're wondering how to pad it out. But this is an old way of looking at non-fiction books, and more to do with traditional publishers who require a certain word count. It might be that your book is fine at a shorter length.

The reverse might also be true, in that the book is already too long and unwieldy. Perhaps you need to break it into shorter books so that you can finish something and make more income from the project.

It's hard work

At this point, you might also be finding the writing harder work than you expected. If that's happening, then welcome to my world! People who haven't written a book expect it to be a simple process to turn thoughts into words on a page. But it's a challenge and it's tiring. Some days you feel like you're in flow and everything is amazing. The next day, every sentence is a grind. But that's not a block – it's the creative process.

Take a break.

If I'm stuck in the middle of a chapter, or just feeling over it, I'll go for a walk. Fresh air cures many ills. But sometimes, if I've been working on something for an extended period of weeks or months, I'll need a bigger break. A few days or weeks away from the manuscript, and you'll come back to the page renewed.

But if you're just procrastinating, stop what you're doing, get your butt into the chair and write.

You've finished a book, and you're not ready to start another one

Perhaps you had a grand plan to write several smaller books on a topic based on the high volume business model described in chapter 2.2. But now you've finished one book, and you're exhausted. You can't imagine writing anything else.

Don't worry. This is normal and it happens to most writers after the end of a book. You have given your all to the manuscript. It's ripped you apart and taken everything. It's natural to feel empty.

It's time to fill the creative well, then trust emergence. If you wait a little, ideas will start to emerge again. Your mind will soon be filled with words waiting to be written.

Whatever the underlying problem, you won't overcome writer's block by moaning about it with author friends for weeks on social media, or by any other distractions. The only way to overcome it is by taking action to fix the underlying issue – then get back to writing.

"I deal with writer's block by lowering my expectations.
I think the trouble starts when you sit down to write and
imagine that you will achieve something magical and
magnificent—and when you don't, panic sets in.

The solution is never to sit down and imagine
that you will achieve something magical and magnificent.
I write a little bit, almost every day, and if it results in two
or three or (on a good day) four good paragraphs,
I consider myself a lucky man. Never try to be the hare.
All hail the tortoise."

Malcolm Gladwell

Questions:

- If you're struggling with your writing, can you identify the reason behind the block?

- How can you deal with this and still achieve your goal of writing a book? What practical steps will you take to move your project forward and still look after yourself?

Resources:

- *Bird by Bird: Some Instructions on Writing and Life* – Anne Lamott

- *Conquering Writer's Block and Summoning Inspiration: Learn to Nurture a Lifestyle of Creativity* – K.M. Weiland

- Interview on How to Banish Writer's Block with K.M. Weiland on The Creative Penn Podcast: www.TheCreativePenn.com/weiland

3.10 Co-writing a non-fiction book

Co-writing is a great way to write a book faster as well as share the load of marketing. You will bring different areas of expertise to the book, and it may make the writing process more fun. I've co-written two non-fiction books, *Co-Writing a Book* with J.Thorn (very meta!), and *The Healthy Writer* with Dr Euan Lawson. I've also co-written five novels, with more on the way, and the process of working with someone else is different every time.

What are the different ways of co-writing?

Your process will depend on the experience of the writers and the way you like to work, but there are two main methods.

(a) Each author takes different sections/chapters and writes separately.

This is how Euan and I worked for *The Healthy Writer*, with each of us owning our different parts and retaining our individual voices throughout.

(b) A/B drafting and revision.

One author takes the primary lead on writing the first draft. The other author goes through and edits, passing over the same material, so one coherent voice is present throughout. The reader will not be able to tell who wrote which section when it is complete.

You can also combine these, taking different approaches per chapter as J. Thorn and I did for *Co-Writing a Book*.

How to find the right person to co-write with

Trust and communication are crucial, so I recommend that you already have some kind of relationship with the person you intend to co-write with. Copyright lasts up to 70 years after the death of the author, so you will be tied together for longer than a marriage. Perhaps you're friends through a writing group, or already writing in the same genre.

It does work best if you are at a similar level of writing ability, so one person isn't doing all the heavy lifting. You can test this out if you're unsure. When Dr Euan Lawson approached me with the idea for *The Healthy Writer*, I asked him to write a test chapter so I could see what his writing was like. As you'd expect from an educated doctor who writes for medical journals, it was well-written, but also quite technical and overly professional. We worked together to help Euan's more informal voice emerge, and then I knew we'd be able to write together.

How to work together effectively

Agree on a contract.

You can find an example in the Appendix of *Co-Writing a Book* or work with an intellectual property lawyer to create one. It's critical to nail down the responsibilities for writing, publishing, marketing, finances and time up front as these are the things that may cause stress later.

Agree working schedules and timelines.

For example, we will both commit to two hours a day, or four completed chapters a week, with the first draft due in four months' time – or whatever works for you.

Emily Thompson and Kathleen Shannon, co-authors of *Being Boss*, scheduled blocks of time to write together even though they lived apart. As Emily discussed in an interview on The Creative Penn Podcast,

"We would get on Zoom together and on Google Docs. We were face to face. So we're basically writing in the same room with each other. We would open up a Google Doc because you can do live writing and live editing, and we would sit there quietly and write the thing, and then we would switch and read each other's. Sometimes we would read our own out loud and workshop it together."

With *The Healthy Writer*, Euan and I agreed on specific checkpoints where we would go through what we had written during a meeting on Skype. We used Google Docs for the draft chapters, up to the point of structuring the book, when we moved everything into Scrivener. Then each of us took ownership of the master file while we worked on it, before handing it back to the other. We went through these iterations several times.

Communication is critical.

Make sure you have regular calls or email for status updates. You could even keep a writing diary, which I did with J. Thorn when we co-wrote together. We worked in different time zones and as introverts, we didn't find speaking a necessity, so we just wrote to each other after every session.

It doesn't matter how you do it – every writing partnership finds its own rhythm. But the most important thing is to agree what you're doing up front, adjust as you go and keep communicating along the way.

Multi-author projects

Co-writing is most often done as a partnership, but anthologies contain separate chapters written by different people. This is common in academia for textbooks and also for collections of essays on a topic. One example would be the *Chicken Soup for the Soul* books.

With multi-author projects, one author needs to take control and act as project manager and central communication point, as well as editing the project for a consistent theme. This type of book can be a logistical challenge, so only take it on if you enjoy organization and working with others.

Questions:

- Are you considering co-writing? Why would it be a good fit for your project?

- Have you identified a potential co-writing partner? Do you already have an existing relationship?

- Do you have a contract in place? Have you agreed on how to split the workload and timings? Have you discussed how things will work in case of success or failure? What is your joint definition of success for this project?

- How will you work together in a practical way? How will you communicate?

- How will you ensure your relationship is preserved in case of difficulty?

Resources:

- *Co-Writing a Book: Collaboration and Co-creation for Authors* – Joanna Penn and J. Thorn

- Chapter on collaborations in *The Self-Publisher's Legal Handbook* – Helen Sedwick

- Article on co-writing mistakes: www.TheCreativePenn.com/cowriting-mistakes

- Interview with J. Thorn on co-writing: www.TheCreativePenn.com/co-writing

- Interview with Dr Euan Lawson on being a healthy writer and how we co-wrote *The Healthy Writer*: www.TheCreativePenn.com/healthy-cowriting

- Interview with Emily Thompson on co-writing *Being Boss*: www.TheCreativePenn.com/beingboss

3.11 How to turn a boring book into an engaging read

One of the challenges for writing non-fiction is to get the balance right. You don't want to write a dry, academic tome, but neither do you want a fluffy book of no substance. You also want to feel that your writing project is a creative experience and not a painful college assignment.

So how can you turn what feels like a boring book into an engaging read?

Share your story and your personal experience in your voice

"What makes non-fiction come alive for me are the personal stories and journal entries to illustrate a point. I love it when I'm reading a non-fiction book in a more conversational tone as if I'm sitting down having a cuppa with a friend and learning something along the way."

Leeza Baric, from The Creative Penn survey

If your book is boring, it's probably because there is no story and no personality in it. You can only bring a subject alive if you make it real by sharing your story.

Talk to the reader as if they were in the room with you. Share your emotion, your heart, your passion, as well as your knowledge.

I came up against these issues when I started writing this book. I felt bogged down in How To information and the writing was boring me and not engaging my creative side at all. Then I took a hard look at why I cared about this project, and how non-fiction has changed my life and impacted my journey. I considered why I love reading and listening to non-fiction, why my bookshelves and my Kindle overflow with non-fiction books.

I went back through my journals and found my notes on various books and the turning points in my life that came after reading them. By sharing those memories, by tapping into that passion, I found the book again. Finishing it became a creative challenge, and I discovered a renewed eagerness for the project. I hope you find the result useful!

Don't be too academic

"Don't use big words. They mean so little."

Oscar Wilde

Don't write like an academic unless you are writing an academic paper or thesis. And if you're writing something like that, then it is not a book. The audience is completely different, and if you do want to turn your thesis into a book, then you need to rewrite it. You are not being assessed or graded by how intelligent you are. You are trying to educate, inspire or entertain a *reader* – not a professor.

Eliminate jargon and remove clichéd phrases that have become over-used in your industry. I used to work in management consultancy, and we would play Bingo at conferences with over-used words like blue-sky thinking, scope creep, quick wins, out of the box, or whenever anyone mentioned a three-letter-acronym (or TLA!). Every industry has these words. You need to decide whether your audience understands them, or if you need to explain them or get rid of them completely.

Use active language and if you're struggling with that, use a tool like Grammarly to identify passive sentence structure, which is particularly common with academic writers.

"Experts writing non-fiction are prone to putting on a posh academic overcoat. The language can be dry, technical, and passive. Work hard to make your prose accessible and tell an engaging story. Shrug off that overcoat and let your passion shine through."

Dr Euan Lawson, my co-writer for The Healthy Writer

Use quotes, images, illustrations, photos or other visuals

You don't have to produce everything from your brain. You can use quotes or visuals that bring your book alive and demonstrate your ideas in new ways.

I like using quotes from books and also from writers who participate in my surveys as it brings in other voices, changes the tone and backs up my thoughts on the topic. I used my own diagrams in *Career Change* to turn the process into visuals. More evidence of my consulting background!

You can hire people on sites like Upwork to create images for you, or you can license images/photos/illustrations if you prefer. Make sure you understand the intellectual property rights around use. Chapter 3.14 covers the legal issues in more detail.

Questions:

- Is your book boring you? Will it bore the reader?

- Have you used academic writing, passive language, or too much jargon?

- What can you do to bring your book alive?

Resources:

- My tutorial on using Grammarly:
  www.TheCreativePenn.com/grammarly-tutorial

- Find freelancers at www.Upwork.com

3.12 Elements of fiction in non-fiction

"There is no longer any such thing as writing fiction or
non-fiction; there's only narrative."

E.L.Doctorow

Yes, you're writing non-fiction, but there are techniques
that you can borrow from fiction writers that will bring
your book alive.

People are interested in people

Great fiction is all about character, because people are
interested in people. You are the main character in your
book, so you need to include personal aspects of your
journey that will enable readers to get a sense of your story
behind the facts.

Obviously, you're not going to make anything up, because
this is non-fiction, but you can dramatize your writing by
'showing, not telling,' as I did in Part 1. I wrote the experience of crying at work and my decision in Bali as if it were
happening, rather than just telling you the result. This
brings life to the book and anchors it in a personal story.

If you conduct interviews for research, you can use dialogue or reported speech to bring aspects of the book alive,
as I have done throughout with excerpts from podcast
interviews. Steven Pressfield also talked about doing this

for *The Lion's Gate* as he described in an interview on The Creative Penn Podcast,

"In non-fiction, you have to go by the rules of storytelling. The book [*The Lion's Gate*] was narrative non-fiction. **I put it together, as an artist would put it together**, and moved one interview here and one interview there, and cut this and cut that, to tell a whole story with recurring characters."

Use a narrative arc

The arc of a story takes a character from where they are at the beginning through the trials and tribulations of what opposes their goal, to an ending where they either triumph or fail. Your book can take the reader on that same arc.

In fact, one of the books that changed my life, *The Success Principles* by Jack Canfield, has a narrative arc in its subtitle: *How to Get From Where You Are To Where You Want To Be*. It implies the story arc for the reader up front and then takes them on that journey. Where does your reader start? Where do you want them to end up? What is the transformation that you will take them through?

Open loops

If you ask a question early on in the book, don't answer it immediately. Keep an open loop in the reader's mind, so they want to read on.

Diet books do this all the time. They have an enticing title and promise at the beginning and then spend the first part outlining all the problems you might be having with your weight, before finally giving you the key at the end. [Spoiler: it's likely to be a variation of eat less, move more!]

Use specific details

"The more you wish to describe a Universal, the more minutely and truthfully you must describe a particular."

Brenda Ueland, If You Want to Write

Writing is a form of manipulation, and in order to do it effectively, you need to control what happens in the reader's head. One way of doing this is to use specific details as opposed to generalities. In *The Healthy Writer*, I tell a personal story about my experience of headache and migraine, using specific details about the sounds, sights and physical sensations of pain.

"Two bars of steel bore through my eyes and the surface of my eyeballs expand from pressure. Light is torture. Pixels split into too much detail, and everything is magnified and in capitals. Sound is amplified to a roar made up of billions of tiny noises all crowding for attention.

Breathing sounds like a deafening waterfall, a footfall is a crash, music a thudding cacophony. There's buzzing in my ears, an insect trying to get out or blood knocking on my brain. My vision narrows as a mask, pink and orange patches dancing on the walls."

Hopefully, you will agree that this is more specific than saying, "I had a headache."

You can also be specific around settings or locations for your story, as I did with sensory detail in the Bali chapter.

If you're bored with your book, the reader will be too, so use some of these techniques to bring your book alive.

"In Bosnian, there's no distinction in literature between fiction and non-fiction; there's no word describing that."

Aleksander Hemon

Questions:

- What elements of fiction could you use to make your book more engaging?

- Where does your reader start? Where do you want them to end up? What is the transformation that you will take them through?

Resources:

- Steven Pressfield on interviews for *The Lion's Gate*, mental toughness and Resistance: www.TheCreativePenn.com/pressfield1

- *If You Want to Write* – Brenda Ueland

3.13 Does non-fiction have to be true?

"You're seeking the truth of memory – your memory and character – not of unbiased history."

Mary Carr, The Art of Memoir

There are many issues of truth when writing non-fiction, and how you address them will depend on the type of book you're writing. Consider these different scenarios.

- You're writing a biography and need to be sure you are exact about the place and year of the subject's birth

- You're writing a book on depression and want to reference specific medical studies about the efficacy of treatment to back up your personal experience

- You're writing a memoir and you're trying to remember which particular episode came first in your personal history

- You're writing self-help and you want to use a personal anecdote but your memory is a little fuzzy on the details

- You want to quote someone but can't remember the exact words they said

Truth is a difficult topic when it comes to personal memory. You will have to decide how far you want to go to find it when writing memoir or self-help because everyone remembers things differently.

Truth can also be difficult when it comes to matters of belief around religion and politics. There are those who would argue their side is true, no matter the evidence for the other.

Then there are things that happened on certain days to certain people that you can check with authoritative sources.

Go beyond Wikipedia to verify dates, quotes, studies, scientific papers and publications. For example, the Appendix of *The Healthy Writer* lists the scientific studies in peer-reviewed medical journals that back up the individual chapters.

But most books are not medical textbooks where the writing on the page may impact life or death.

Most books are not investigative journalism where every cited source is critical. If you're paralyzed by the need to make sure every single thing is double and triple checked, perfectionism may kill your book before it ever reaches the world. So be careful not to spend years in research checking every little thing.

Of course, it is your responsibility to make sure you've checked everything *if* your book does depend on this type of research. Provide the right information for your book and care enough about your audience that you do your best to make sure everything is correct.

Questions:

- What are the important things that need to be right in your book and what can be included for the sake of story and impact?

Resources:

- *The Art of Memoir* – Mary Carr

3.14 Legal issues: Using real people, quotes, lyrics, images and citing sources

Disclaimer: I am not a lawyer, and this is not legal advice. This chapter is an overview from my perspective based on questions that authors ask all the time. Please check the books listed in the Resources section below for more detail.

Copyrighting your work

"Copyright is a legal device that provides the creator of a work of art or literature, or a work that conveys information or ideas, the right to control how the work is used."

Stephen Fishman, The Copyright Handbook

Copyright law grants authors specific rights over their work including the right to make copies (reproduction), distribution, adaptation, as well as performance and display rights. Those rights can only be used by the author, or by another person or entity to whom rights are granted.

You cannot copyright an idea, but the unique expression of the idea belongs to you, in this case, a draft manuscript or book.

It is your copyright whether you add the © symbol or not. The Berne convention protects copyright across different countries, and usually, copyright lasts for 50-70 years after the death of the author, but this differs based on the work and the country it is published in.

You don't have to register the work for copyright to be applied, but there may be benefits to doing so in certain countries. Look up 'copyright registration + your country' to find the appropriate service.

It's important to understand copyright, as it gives your work value and is the basis of any publishing contracts you sign.

Your book is not just one manuscript.

It can be licensed in almost unlimited ways, for example, an audiobook in English, a print book in French sold in France and Belgium only, an audiobook in Arabic, or turned into a screenplay and made into a documentary for Netflix. Each of these examples requires different licensing of your copyright, but many authors don't read their contracts and sign away everything without understanding the value they hold.

If you consider how important your original work can be for you, it will also help you understand the importance of permissions for other people's copyrighted work.

Using quotes

Many non-fiction writers use quotes from other books. These usually come under the terms of 'fair use,' which permits limited use of copyrighted material without needing permission for the purposes of commentary, criticism, education or parody.

So you can quote a few lines from this book with attribution without my permission, but you can't copy and paste a whole chapter into your book or blog to use verbatim.

Some written work will be in the public domain, or the copyright will have expired, for example, Shakespeare's plays, which means that you can use the whole work. But be careful, as translations of older works are often still in copyright. The Bible in the original Hebrew or Greek might be in the public domain, but modern translations are likely still under copyright. Make sure you check before use.

Using lyrics

Songs are shorter works, so even if you quote one line, you're likely to go over the limited definition of fair use unless the song is in the public domain. It's best to avoid lyrics unless you get permission, which can take time and potentially be expensive. Song titles are not copyrighted, but lyrics are, so be careful.

Generally, it's best to avoid lyrics.

For more detail and a sample permission letter, see *How to use Memorable Lyrics without Paying a Fortune or a Lawyer*, by Helen Sedwick and Jessica M. Brown.

Using images

If you want to use photos, diagrams, cartoons, or other images within your book or on the cover that you don't explicitly own, then you need to make sure that you have licensed the image for the specific purpose, or that it is in the public domain.

Don't ever download an image off the Internet and use it freely on your site or in your book. The big image banks like Getty have algorithms that check for usage, and you may end up inadvertently infringing copyright and getting a bill for thousands of dollars.

Most authors will use royalty-free images from sites like BigStockPhoto, iStockPhoto or Shutterstock. Some sites permit unlimited use, but some have limits, e.g. 250,000 downloads. That might seem a lot, but if you use an image on the cover of a free ebook, you might hit that sooner than you think.

If you want to use a specific image, for example, a historical picture that fits with your book, then you can request permission to use it from the rights holder and agree on a fee.

For more detail and sample permission letter, see *How to use Eye-Catching Images without Paying a Fortune or a Lawyer* by Helen Sedwick and Jessica Brown.

Writing about real people

If you're writing happy, positive things about people that are historically accurate, then you probably don't need to worry. But that's not usually why writers include real people in their books!

If you're writing about people who are alive and what you're writing may damage their reputation or livelihood, embarrass them or attract negative public attention, then you need to consider possible legal ramifications around the invasion of privacy and/or defamation.

You also need to consider the impact your book might have on people you care about, even if the people written about are not directly involved.

Consider whether you need to disguise people involved completely, use a pseudonym, or perhaps even fictionalize the story.

"If you're doing it for therapy, go hire somebody to talk to. Your psychic health should matter more than your literary production. If you want revenge, hire a lawyer."

Mary Carr, The Art of Memoir

Citing sources

You should always cite your sources, whether that is a conversation or a podcast or a book or however you came by the information. Don't claim something is yours if you came across it elsewhere.

Regarding format for citations, it will depend on the type of book you're writing and the format you're publishing in. You can just refer to the person or book within the text. Many mass market non-fiction books will also include a Bibliography or Appendices with citations by chapter, as we did for *The Healthy Writer*, which lists medical references used within the book.

Academic books tend to use footnotes and specific citation layout as outlined in *The Chicago Manual of Style* and other style guides. But remember that these can be difficult for people reading on ebooks and audiobooks, so you might need to change things by format.

Avoid plagiarism

Plagiarism is stealing other people's work and portraying it as your own, either by directly copying their words or by taking an expression of an idea and reproducing it in a very similar way.

This is just as relevant online as it is in published work, for example, copying and pasting other people's blog posts into your site is plagiarism.

It is not plagiarism to read other people's books, quote them in your own and write your book on the same topic. I've read a lot of books on writing non-fiction, but you won't find one exactly like this because it's my original work, my expression of the idea. I've also cited my sources when I've referred to other people's work, giving them credit and directing you to their books and resources. Most writers appreciate being quoted in this way, as it can be great marketing.

Most writers would never plagiarize deliberately, but it is easy to accidentally plagiarize when writing non-fiction, especially if you copy and paste chunks of text during the research process. These blocks of text may find their way into your finished book unless you watch out for them.

There are two main ways to check for this. When self-editing your book, print it out and read it through, noting any parts that don't sound like your voice. You should be able to spot them quite easily. If your whole book sounds stilted, then revisit chapter 1.4 on finding your voice. If anything stands out as writing that doesn't sound like you, rewrite it. You can also use a tool like Grammarly, which has an automated plagiarism checker.

Don't let these things stop you from writing

This chapter is an overview of *possible* legal issues associated with writing non-fiction, but don't let concerns around this stop you from writing.

Write the book you want to write. No one will see that first draft anyway, so you can do whatever you want with it. Then review the draft and see whether you have to worry about anything. Make changes if you need to, or secure the permissions to use other material, or work with a lawyer to check the manuscript if you are still worried.

I've written nine non-fiction books and have never had any issues. I've been pragmatic and avoided the use of lyrics or other people's images/illustrations, even if I've wanted to use them. Readers are not going to notice their absence, so if in doubt, leave them out.

Questions:

- Do you understand copyright and the value of your intellectual property?

- Are you using quotes, lyrics, or images that you don't specifically own? Do you have the specific licenses or permission to use them?

- Are you writing about real people? Could there be any legal or personal ramifications of this?

- Have you attributed quotes or ideas within your book? Have you cited your sources?

- Have you checked for inadvertent plagiarism?

- If you're still worried, have you checked through the Resources below or worked with an attorney around what you include in the book?

Resources:

- *The Self-Publisher's Legal Handbook* – Helen Sedwick

- *The Copyright Handbook: What Every Writer Needs to Know* – Stephen Fishman

- *Closing the Deal…On Your Terms: Agents, Contracts, and Other Considerations* – Kristine Kathryn Rusch

- *How to use Memorable Lyrics without Paying a Fortune or a Lawyer* – Helen Sedwick and Jessica M. Brown

- *How to use Eye-Catching Images without Paying a Fortune or a Lawyer* – Helen Sedwick and Jessica Brown

- *The Chicago Manual of Style* – University of Chicago Press

- Grammarly plagiarism checker and editing software: www.TheCreativePenn.com/grammarly

- Legal issues blog for writers: www.HelenSedwick.com

- Creative Law Center: www.CreativeLawCenter.com

- Interview with attorney, Helen Sedwick, on copyright, publishing contract clauses, image use, and avoiding getting sued: www.TheCreativePenn.com/helen

3.15 Self-editing a book

"In anything at all, perfection is finally attained not when there is no longer anything to add, but when there is no longer anything to take away."

Antoine de Saint Exupéry

You have finished the first draft when you can print it out and read it end to end without missing sections. It is the raw material that you can now shape into the finished book. I don't recommend that you share your first draft with anyone, but wait until you have at least done this first self-edit, as you will find it much improves your work in progress.

My self-editing process

I find printing out my first draft to be the most effective way of self-editing, as it turns words on the screen into something that more resembles a book. I will often 'rest' the manuscript at this point, leaving it in a folder until I feel less emotionally connected to it and able to tackle the text with a clear mind. This usually takes a week or so.

I schedule blocks of time for editing, then work old-school with a biro to scribble notes, draw arrows to move things around, write extra material, change words, and delete lines, as well as completing any placeholders like [insert explanation here]. Some pages end up as a mass of black marks, others are relatively clean. But no page goes untouched.

Of course, you can use a computer screen or tablet, but I'd suggest at least changing the font, so there is some difference to when you were writing. It's always difficult to see our own errors.

This first round of editing is more about structure, missing sections, and big issues than it is about grammar and sentence structure, although of course, you will pick those up, too.

When you read the manuscript end to end, you may discover that the order of the chapters is wrong, or you need a quote for this section, or you need to rewrite a whole segment to make it clearer. This process is completely normal, and this first edit is likely to be the major one, as you hack the text into something closer to the end goal.

I then type those hand-written changes back into my Scrivener project and make more updates as I go. If the changes are significant, I will then print out the manuscript again and do another round of hand-edits.

In this first self-edit, aim to improve the manuscript in the following ways.

Make the reader's journey through the book as clear and easy as possible

Words are a form of time travel and telepathy. The words you write down on a page are transmitted into another person's brain at a different point in time and space. But you won't be there to explain what you meant if the reader is confused. Unlike a blog post or social media chat, there is no real-time interaction around a book. It's your job to make the book as clear as possible, so there are no outstanding questions.

Does the chapter flow take the reader logically through a journey of discovery and transformation? What would make it stronger? Are you using jargon without explaining it? Can you use sub-headings to make sections clearer? Can you involve the reader by asking more questions?

Cut it down

> "Examine every word you put on paper. You'll find a surprising number that don't serve any purpose."
>
> *William Zinsser, On Writing Well*

You will likely find that you have repeated yourself at different times, so get rid of anything you have said more than once. Cut down over-wordy sentences to make your point clearer. Don't worry about word count, as one of the most common complaints about non-fiction is that it is 'over-padded.' Short books with clear benefits to the reader are better than longer ones that the reader has to wade through to find the gold.

Make it more personal

If some chapters are too info-dense, or the book is lacking in personality, then add in more of your story and experience. You can also use quotes per section to bring in different voices. I like to use excerpts from my journals, as well as appropriate quotes I've collected. In *The Healthy Writer*, we used quotes from a reader survey, bringing multiple new voices to the text.

You might read over some sections and feel that they don't sound like your voice. If this happens, you may have inadvertently copied something from another book, so make sure you reword anything that doesn't sound like you in order to avoid plagiarism.

"Good writing does not succeed or fail on the strength of its ability to persuade. It succeeds or fails on the strength of its ability to engage you, to make you think, to give you a glimpse into someone else's head."

Malcolm Gladwell

Check your facts and quotes. Add references or extra bonus material.

Have you kept a list of your references and included that in an Appendix?

You can complete this section later, but it's best to check facts as you go, collect references, and put things together in draft form as you edit. Trust me on this! It will be a lot more work if you leave it to the last minute and have to scour through everything trying to find where you quoted from.

You can also consider extra material at this stage. How can you make the book even more useful? Can you make downloadable extras or checklists? How about audio snippets or videos that will help the reader even more?

Use Grammarly to improve the draft

Once I've finished my edits, I copy and paste each chapter into Grammarly editing software. It picks up passive voice, repetitive words, incorrect comma usage, typos, and bad sentence structure, and even has a plagiarism checker. I could leave all this to my editor or proofreader, but I want to hand over a clean manuscript so they can look for other issues on their pass through. I also learn more if I go through this process, which improves my writing for the next book.

You will likely have a 'writer's tic,' sometimes more than one, and it can be hard to spot these for yourself. I overuse words like very, own, or actually, and have to remove them in my self-edit.

Read the book out loud

If you want to check that the book makes sense, try reading it aloud. It's easy to spot bulky sentences this way, so it's particularly useful if you come from an academic background and are prone to writing at length. If you intend to turn the manuscript into an audiobook, this can be a useful exercise to determine what might not work when read aloud, for example, long lists of bullet points, URLs, or diagrams.

When have you completed a self-edit?

When you feel that you cannot improve the book anymore, rest the manuscript again. Put it away for a week or two and try to forget about it. Then print it out and read it through once more. You will find more to improve, but of course you have to balance the need for perfection with getting your book out into the world.

When you really can't do anymore, it's time to work with a professional editor and proofreader.

Questions:

- Have you set aside time for your self-editing process? Have you printed out the manuscript or created a new version with a different font on your computer so it looks different to the original?

- Is the reader's journey through the book as clear and easy as possible? Does the chapter flow take the reader logically through a journey of discovery and transformation?

- Can you cut down the text anymore? Can you use sub-headings to make sections clearer? Can you involve the reader by asking more questions? Can you make the book more personal by telling your story and bringing in your experience?

- Have you checked your facts and cited sources? Have you listed your references and bibliography? Do you need to create any bonus material?

- Have you checked the draft using software like Grammarly, or reading it aloud?

- Have you done everything you can to improve the manuscript? Are you ready to work with a professional editor or proofreader?

Resources:

- Grammarly editing software:
  www.TheCreativePenn.com/grammarly

- My Grammarly tutorial:
  www.TheCreativePenn.com/grammarly-tutorial

- *On Writing Well* – William Zinsser

3.16 How to find and work with professional editors and proofreaders

At this point in the process, you will not be able to see your manuscript objectively anymore. You might even be completely over it and never want to read another word. This is normal, and it means you're ready for the next stage.

Why work with a professional editor?

If you want your book to be the best it can be, then working with an editor is the best way to do that.

An editor's job is to take your raw manuscript and improve it – whether that be through structural changes, line edits, suggestions of new material or sentence refinement. A professional editor has experience in shaping manuscripts, and they will see your mistakes clearly, as well as know how to fix them. While you are mired in the weeds, they can take a bird's eye view of your work and pinpoint what will improve it.

You will also learn from a professional editor and improve your craft based on their feedback. You can carry those lessons into your next book, so it's an investment in your writing future. It might also mean that the first edit is the most significant, as you have the most to learn, but we all have to start somewhere!

Importantly, the editor should not fundamentally change your book. They should shape it into a better version of itself, retaining your voice and ideas while at the same time, improving it for the reader. This is a skillful balancing act, which is why experienced editors are so highly prized!

What if they steal my work?

This is a common concern of new writers who think that editors will run away with their book and make millions with their idea. But don't worry! Editors are professionals, and they work within a contractual framework that protects both parties.

You can also register your copyright first if you are concerned about this, as covered in chapter 3.14.

Different types of editor

There are several broad categories of editor.

A **structural or developmental editor** will work with you at a high level to shape the book into a coherent flow. They will read your manuscript and then provide a report about content organization, missing sections, tone and voice, as well as suggestions for improvement.

A **technical editor** is a specialist in a particular field, and they will focus only on verifying their area of expertise.

A **copy editor or line editor** focuses on improving sentences, grammar, and style, as well as suggesting other ways of rephrasing ideas. They may also provide comments on anything else they pick up.

Non-fiction books often use particular styles, for example, chapter headings, sub-headings, action points, bullet points, call-outs and examples, so these may be checked too. The copy editor will usually use Track Changes on MS Word. This is the classic 'red pen' edit where you can expect a lot of changes.

A **proofreader** checks the manuscript line by line in the stage before publication. You should have made any changes based on previous editing rounds, and then the proofreader is the final check. They should not find anything significant at this stage but will note typos or incorrect use of words, inconsistencies in formatting, and other specific details.

You don't need all these editors for every book you write.

It will depend on your situation. If you're struggling with organizing your content, consider working with a structural editor. If you've never written a book before, working with a copy editor is a good idea as you will have a lot to learn. And personally, I never publish a book without using a proofreader!

Beta readers

These are readers in your target market who read the book and offer comments on the content. They are not professional editors, so you can't expect them to pick up structural or grammatical issues, but they can be useful for feedback.

I gave an early copy of *Career Change* to people working in my department at my day job who I knew were dissatisfied with what they were doing. They came back with questions and suggestions for what to include as additional material.

How to find a professional editor

Most authors will credit their editors and proofreaders in the Acknowledgments section of their books, so if there is a particular book that you have enjoyed, then check out whether you can hire their editor. Many editors will have websites and write articles or feature on podcasts, so you can easily find editors once you start looking.

Check my recommended list:

www.TheCreativePenn.com/editors

Check whether the editor has experience in and enjoys your genre. This is critical because expectations will be different across the board. You don't want a scientific editor working with you on your memoir.

Make sure the editor has testimonials from happy authors, and check directly with a named client if you want to take it further. Some editors will do a test edit on one chapter, which helps both parties decide whether working together is appropriate.

Many editors are booked up months in advance, so once you have your plan in place, contact them early and book a slot. Make sure to update them if your timings change.

How much does an editor cost?

This will depend on what type of edit you require, your word count, how experienced you are as a writer, and how much experience the editor has. There is no standard amount. Each editor will quote rates on their website, so check this or ask for a quote when you do your research.

The self-editing process should help keep your costs down by ensuring you have done a lot of the work yourself before submission.

Every dollar I have spent on editing has been worth it, and I continue to use editors/proofreaders for all of my books. The more eyes on your book before publication, the better it will be on launch.

What if you have a tight budget?

Working with a professional is always the best choice, so if possible, save up to work with an editor. It's an investment in your future writing career. But of course, if you really can't afford it, there are some other options.

You can barter with other writers in the same genre, editing each other's work, or providing services you might be more skilled at, e.g. help with marketing tasks.

You could workshop your writing in a writer's group, but I'm personally wary of 'writing by committee,' and this may impact your voice, the thing that makes you special.

You can also work with beta readers, some of whom may have deep knowledge in a niche, and may be able to offer great feedback.

How to work with an editor

When you engage an editor of any kind, you should receive a contract with a timeline as well as a price for the work. You will need to deliver the manuscript on a particular date and will usually pay a deposit, especially if this is the first time you're working together. The editor will agree to deliver the edits back on a certain date.

There may be provision to have a call to discuss the work, or you may receive a structural report, line edit, or proofread manuscript by email. I've worked with professional editors for the last ten years and have never had a call to discuss, but if you're the type of person who wants that, then make sure you include it in the contract up front along with anything else you're concerned about.

If you have questions about the editing process, now is the time to ask.

This is a two-way relationship, and you need to behave as professionally as the editor should. Any issues can usually be avoided by communicating expectations up front and getting the contract sorted out early.

Once the preliminaries are agreed, submit the manuscript to your editor – usually by email in MS Word format. They will return it to you on the agreed timeline with Track Changes and any other documents, e.g. structural report, style sheet, other notes.

When you receive that email, particularly if it's your first book, make sure you are well rested and in a positive frame of mind before you open it.

If it's your first book, the editing process will be hard on your ego.

Remember, the editor's job is to make your manuscript better and help you learn the craft. You are paying them to give you critical feedback, not pat you on the back and say 'good job.'

If you have an emotional reaction to the comments, don't email back immediately. Let the comments rest with you for a few days, and then you will find it easier to accept them.

Once you are ready, go through the manuscript and update your Master file, which for me, is always my Scrivener project. I'd suggest working through each change so you can learn for next time, rather than just clicking Accept All on the Track Changes version. This will take time, but it's well worth it.

I usually accept 80-90% of my editor's changes and the manuscript is improved considerably by the experience. After the line edits are updated, I send the manuscript to a proofreader for the final check before publication.

* * *

Congratulations! You now have a completed manuscript. Let's get into the publishing process.

Questions:

- Why is working with a professional editor a good idea?

- What are the different types of editor and which ones will you consider for your manuscript?

- How will you find a professional editor and validate that they are the right one for you?

- How will you work with your editor so that you are both happy with the process and the result?

- How can you prepare yourself mentally for receiving your edited manuscript? How can you reframe the experience as positive and learn for next time?

- How will you celebrate completing your manuscript?

Resources:

- My list of recommended editors:
  www.TheCreativePenn.com/editors

- My tutorial video on how to find and work with professional editors:
  www.TheCreativePenn.com/editor-tutorial

Part 4:
Publishing
and Product
Creation

4.1 Your publishing options

"It provides some kind of primal verification:
you are in print; therefore, you exist."

Anne Lamott, Bird by Bird

This is not a book on publishing – and I won't be going through how to find an agent or a publisher, or how to self-publish in detail. For the latter, check out my book, *Successful Self-Publishing: How to Self-Publish and Market Your Book*. But to help you start to consider your options, this chapter covers the pros and cons of traditional publishing and self-publishing.

Authors now have a choice in how they publish and get their books into the hands of readers. Many non-fiction authors, in particular, choose to self-publish because they already have a market to sell to.

Some authors are now 'hybrid,' using different forms of publishing for different projects. Hopefully, this chapter will help you evaluate your options.

What is traditional publishing?

Traditional publishing refers to the established system of getting a book deal, which involves submission of your book proposal and/or manuscript to agents over a period of time, some rejections, and then possibly being signed.

The agent will then submit your proposal/manuscript to publishers with a number of rejections, and then (hopefully) a contract is signed. The book will go through more edits and will eventually be published.

The benefits of traditional publishing

Prestige, kudos and validation

Most authors suffer from self-doubt and wonder if their work is good enough. If you make it through the process to get an agent and then a publisher, approval by these gate-keepers can be validation that your work is 'good enough.' If your definition of success includes a traditional deal for these reasons, then go for it!

Print distribution in bookstores is easier

Traditional publishing excels at print distribution, and their business model is primarily designed around it. Sales reps go around bookstores, and buyers select books they want and pay later with one invoice per publisher minus any returns. Books are usually in the store for a month to six weeks and only remain if they are perennial sellers.

You will have an established professional team to work with

Your editors, cover designer, formatter, and (possibly) marketing help is provided as part of the publishing con-tract. Marketing effort is related to how much the publisher has invested in the project, and marketing for publishing companies is usually to booksellers rather than consumers.

There are no up-front financial costs, and you should get an advance against royalties

You don't have to pay anyone to get a traditional publishing deal and if you are asked for money, then it is NOT a traditional publishing deal. The median author advance is currently around £6000 or US$10,000. Increasingly, there are now deals where the author will take higher royalties and a smaller advance, or no advance at all.

Remember that the advance is against royalties, which are usually 7-25% of net book price. So if you get an advance of $10,000, you then have to earn more than $10,000 out of your royalty rate on book sales before you get any more money.

Literary prizes and critical acclaim

These are more likely through traditional publishing, and many literary prizes aren't even open to indie authors. There have been outliers, e.g. *A Naked Singularity* by Sergio De Le Pava, which won the PEN/Robert W Bingham Prize, but it's still rare for self-published authors to be allowed to enter literary prizes.

The downsides of traditional publishing

Loss of creative control

You generally give this up when you sign with a publisher. Many authors get titles, covers and marketing angles that they're not happy with. Check your contract for how much input you will be able to have.

An incredibly slow process

Writing and editing will be the same regardless of how you want to publish. But then it might take you a year or two to get an agent. Then it might take a year to get a publishing deal and then it will likely be another year before you launch your book.

So it's a very, very slow process, which is crazy in a world where you can self-publish, and have your book on sale within four hours and then payment 60 days later.

Low royalty rates

Royalty rates are a percentage of the sale of the book. They're likely to be net, so all the discounts, returns, marketing costs and overheads are taken off the total before your percentage is calculated. Royalty rates for traditional publishing will usually range between 7% and 25%, although some digital-first publishers are now offering higher ebook royalties.

Rates also differ by format, e.g. ebook vs. hardback vs. audio. Royalty reports may come every six months for a specific period of sales, and many authors report how difficult they are to understand. They may also not tally with the amount of money that you receive, so traditionally published authors can't do an accurate cash flow forecast for future income.

Lack of significant marketing help

Increasingly, authors have to do their own marketing and agents will often seek out authors who have a 'platform' or at least an email list of readers. This is particularly common with non-fiction authors. If you do want a traditional pub-lishing deal, make sure you find out what is included for marketing and make sure you get more than just inclusion in a bookstore catalog.

Potentially prohibitive contract clauses

Getting an agent and a publisher is like a marriage. You don't plan for it to fail, but sometimes the situation just doesn't work out. (And I say that as someone who is very happily married – for the second time!)

You want to be able to get out of this relationship if it goes south, or if the publisher just isn't selling enough of your books and you think you can do a better job. Because once you sign a contract for your book, it belongs to the publisher, and it may belong to the publisher for the life of the copyright, which is the life of the author plus 70 years after you die.

That is a really big deal! So be careful what you sign.

Check your agency contract

A few years ago, I had two New York agencies interested in representing me, so I went through their initial contracts. One of them included a clause where the agency would receive 15% of *everything* I published, regardless of whether they sold the work or not, and that included self-published work. They said that they would build my author brand, so they would be responsible for my success. I've spent years building my platform and my brand, and so I went with the other agency who had a simple clause that specified they didn't receive any sales from my self-published work, only from books they sold. Seems fair to me.

Be careful of signing away World English rights in all formats

Your job and your agent's job, if you have one, is to keep as many rights as possible when you're doing a deal so you can exploit them in other ways. For example, you could license US and Canada rights, then self-publish in the rest of the world. It's highly unlikely that your publisher will publish your book in every country in the world, whereas you can self-publish in 190 countries. So hold onto any territory they do not intend to exploit.

Be careful with the formats included in the contract. Many publishers take audio rights as part of a contract but don't produce an audiobook. Either keep audio rights or specify a length of time the publisher has in which to exploit them before the rights revert to you.

Check the term of the contract and the rights reversion clause

It used to be that there was an out of print clause, but of course, in these days of print-on-demand and ebooks, a book never goes out of print. You have to consider when you might get your rights back, in case things go wrong.

Check the do not compete clause

This may stop you publishing during the term of the contract under the same name, in a similar niche.

Publishers are not charities

They're not doing you a favor by publishing your book. They are businesses, and they want to make money. Remember how important your rights are over the long term. Many authors will sign deals because they're grateful that they were offered anything, but you need to value your work.

To put this into perspective, consider these questions:

- Think of your favorite book

- What is the author's name?

- What is the publisher's name?

Most people will have a favorite book and they'll know the name of the author, but they are unlikely to know the name of the publisher. Most readers don't shop by publisher. Publishers and publishing names and imprints only mean something to authors and those in the industry. Are you writing to impress other authors or to reach readers? Either is valid, but you need to know what you're aiming for.

So your publishing choice is more a question of the outcome that you want to achieve and your definition of success. It's not really what the reader thinks about.

Would I take a traditional publishing deal?

Absolutely. For the right project and for the right terms and conditions.

But I'm a businesswoman and a creative entrepreneur so personally, I choose not to spend my energy chasing these deals. I choose to write the books I want, when I want, and get them into readers' hands as soon as possible, retaining full control. I'm primarily an indie author, so let's now look at the pros and cons of self-publishing.

The difference between self-publishing and being an indie author

The term 'self-publishing' implies doing everything yourself and doing it more as a hobby, rather than a business. There's certainly nothing wrong with this and it's wonderful to produce books for the love of creation. I self-publish photo-books for my own pleasure, I helped my 9-year-old niece self-publish her first book and I helped my Dad self-publish for his 65th birthday.

But I use the term independent author, or indie author, for what I do. I work with freelance professionals to create quality products, and this is my business, not a hobby. I make a multiple six-figure income as an author entrepreneur, and being an indie is a positive choice for me, not a last resort.

The benefits of being an indie author

Total creative control over content and design

Many authors who were in traditional publishing and are now indie talk about how painful it was to have a cover or title they hated, or to have editorial choices imposed on them that they didn't agree with but were insisted upon.

As an indie, you can work with freelancers of your choice and you can choose the ultimate look and feel of your product. You can also change it, as I have done by re-titling and re-covering several of my books.

Many non-fiction authors already run their own businesses and are used to making their own decisions, which is why so many of them choose to go the indie route with their books.

Empowerment

The *Journal of Personality and Social Psychology* reported that the number one contributor to happiness is autonomy, "the feeling that your life – its activities and habits – are under your control." After signing a contract, traditionally published authors have pretty much zero control – over pricing, timing of publication, marketing, sometimes over the cover, the title and even the words themselves.

Plenty of authors are told to change their books to fit what a publisher wants. Compare that to the empowerment of the indie author, who can learn new skills, work with professionals, make mistakes and learn from them, earn money directly and interact with customers. Yes, it's hard work, but it's certainly empowering. The positive energy involved in being an indie can propel you much further, much faster than waiting in line for your turn.

Stop asking permission. You don't need it.

Stop waiting to be chosen. Choose yourself.

Faster time to market

You still have to spend the same amount of time writing and editing. But once you're ready to publish, you can upload your files and your ebook is usually for sale within 24-72 hours. You're paid 60 days after the end of the month of sale.

If you're doing print-on-demand, you can make it available within 24 hours if you approve the formatting online. Or, you can order a proof copy and it might take a couple of weeks, but essentially, it's incredibly quick to get your book up for sale.

This certainly suits my personality, as once I'm done with a book, I want it out there and selling! I don't want to sit on it for several years while it shuttles around the publishing system.

Higher royalties

If you price your book between $2.99 and $9.99 (on Amazon), you can get a 70% royalty, and some of the other stores don't have a price cap on the 70% option. Traditional royalty rates are usually 7-25%. You need to sell far fewer books in order to make the same amount of money as an indie.

But it's certainly not a get-rich-quick scheme. That's really important. You can't guarantee that you're going to make as many sales as you would have done with a traditional publisher, or indeed, any sales at all. That's more to do with genre, investment in marketing and sometimes pure luck. An author can't build a business on luck – but they can learn about marketing, and authors have to do that these days, regardless of how they publish. If you already have a platform, you'll be driving sales regardless of how you publish.

Sell by any means in any global market, as you retain the rights

My books have now sold in 89 countries and they're for sale in 190 countries. I sell direct from my website as well as through the online distributors. The bulk of sales are still US, UK, Canada and Australia, but the global sales are slowly increasing. Over the next few years, mobile penetration, and faster Internet access, as well as potential AI translation, will make it easier to sell in global markets.

This is for books in English, which is currently the most international language for reading. Many traditionally published authors have sold World English rights for all formats and yet have barely sold outside their own country markets because their books aren't even available in most places in the world.

If you're in this situation, revisit your contract. What do you have the rights for? You can always self-publish in countries where you haven't sold the rights, so why not get on with it!

Niche books can reach an audience

Publishing houses have an expectation of a certain number of sales, so if you're writing a niche book on a particular type of organic tomato, you might find the market is too small for a major publisher. But the market size may well be enough for you to satisfy your own definition of success with smaller sales and lower income. You can also price as you like, as chances are that your book will appeal to a very particular reader who might pay higher prices.

Use it to get into the game

These days, if you self-publish and do well, agents and publishers will come to you. You don't have to beg and plead for attention. The power balance is reversed and the empowered indie can get much better deals than a first-time author with no evidence of sales.

The downsides of being an indie author

So there's the positive side, but what about the negatives?

You need to do it all yourself or find suitable professionals to help

As with any new skill, it's a steep learning curve. You still have to do the writing and marketing, but you also have to do the publishing. You have to find an editor and a cover designer and work with them, decide on the title, get your work formatted into ebook, print and any other format you want and find suitable professionals to help.

This isn't such a big deal as we all share with each other online and you can join The Alliance of Independent Authors, which vets companies who can help you. But you do have to decide on your definition of success and understand that you need to run all aspects of the business if you want to go the indie route.

For many people, this is a negative, because they just don't have the time to do everything or they don't enjoy doing it. But I love being an entrepreneur and I enjoy all aspects of what I do – from idea generation to creating words on the page, to the technical side of things and everything in between. Many non-fiction authors have this preference, too.

So, if you can manage a project or you're happy to learn, then you'll likely enjoy it. But this life is certainly not for everyone.

There's no prestige, kudos or validation by the industry

This is not such a big deal in non-fiction, as so many authors are going indie now and the stigma lessens every day. But if your definition of success is bound up with what other authors, agents and publishers think of you, indie might not be the best route.

You need a budget up front if you want a professional result

These days, you're likely to spend on professional editing before submitting to an agent anyway, or at least be spending on books and courses for writers. If, like me, you're intending to make a living from this, then you need to invest money in creating intellectual property assets for the business with the intention of getting it back in multiple streams of income. Either way, you will need a budget up front if you want to be a professional indie author.

It's difficult to get print distribution in bookstores

It's certainly not impossible and if you care about print distribution then look at options with Ingram Spark or work with a printing and distribution company in your target area. But you're much more likely to get bookstore distribution with a traditional publisher, as that's essentially their business model and has been for a long time. They are experts at printing and distributing physical product.

My personal choice is to use print-on-demand through Createspace and IngramSpark, so my print books are available on all online bookstores, and bookstores/universities/libraries can easily order them.

Most literary prizes don't accept indie books and most literary critics for mainstream media won't review them

So if your definition of success is literary acclaim, you're probably better off going the traditional route, although things are changing and prizes are opening up to indie authors, albeit slowly.

The hybrid model: It's not an either/or choice anymore

The industry has changed and many authors now take a hybrid approach to publishing. They will make the decision by book and by particular rights, using the indie model for some things and taking traditional deals for others. This empowers the author to make decisions and choose the best possible route for each project. After all, a career isn't built on one book.

The important thing is that you, the creator, are empowered to choose per project how you would like to progress.

What if you want help with publishing?

Some people find ebook and print book publishing too much of a hassle and would rather pay someone else to do it for them. That's fine and of course, it's up to you how much work you want to do yourself.

Publishing these days is not just a binary choice between traditional publishing and self-publishing. There are myriad options along the scale and lots of companies that can help you. Many of these companies are fantastic but some of them are sharks, so be careful.

Spend a couple of dollars and save yourself thousands

Buy *Choosing A Self-Publishing Service* by the Alliance of Independent Authors, available on all the ebook stores. It's a guide to self-publishing services written by authors, for authors, with no vested interest in the companies described.

The Alliance also has a watchdog listing of companies and whether they are recommended or not. Find it at:

www.TheCreativePenn.com/watchdog

You can also join the Alliance and take advantage of the collective knowledge, as well as becoming part of a growing community. I'm a Member and Advisor and I do monthly sessions with the founder, Orna Ross, plus they have a weekly podcast to help authors.

Find out more about the Alliance of Independent Authors:

www.TheCreativePenn.com/alliance

If you are considering a publishing company, do your research

Make sure that you know what you're getting into and what the costs are, not just to publish but also to make changes to your file.

Check the contract carefully in terms of the rights you might be assigning and how much control you will have in the process. How much are the royalties and when are they paid?

You're likely to be excited about getting your book into the world now, but you still want to be excited in the future. Try to make your publishing choice a business decision, not just an emotional one.

Recommended service: BookBaby

If you don't want to learn how to self-publish yourself, there are many companies who will help you get your book into the world.

BookBaby is a good combination of great service ethic and good value in terms of a managed publishing service. I interviewed the CEO, Steven Spatz, and he outlined how much their team enjoy helping authors with the project management side.

BookBaby offer editing, cover design, formatting, book marketing options, ebook publishing, print-on-demand publishing, wholesale printing, and more. They are a Partner Member of the Alliance of Independent Authors, so they pass muster with the watchdog service.

You can get 10% off at BookBaby if you use my link:

www.TheCreativePenn.com/bookbaby

or just go to BookBaby.com

Questions:

- What are the pros and cons of traditional publishing?

- What are the pros and cons of becoming an indie author?

- Which publishing option relates to your definition of success and will help you achieve your goals?

- What are the things you should watch out for before you sign a contract?

- Have you checked that the company you want to work for is recommended by authors?

Resources:

- *Closing the Deal on your Terms: Agents, Contracts and Other Considerations* – Kristine Katherine Rusch

- *How Authors Sell Publishing Rights* – Orna Ross and Helen Sedwick

- *Successful Self-Publishing: How to Self-Publish and Market Your Book* – Joanna Penn

- *Choosing A Self-Publishing Service* – The Alliance of Independent Authors

- The Alliance of Independent Authors Watchdog listing of publishing companies: www.TheCreativePenn.com/watchdog

- Find out more about the Alliance of Independent Authors: www.TheCreativePenn.com/alliance

- Interview with Steven Spatz, CEO of BookBaby about self-publishing options: www.TheCreativePenn.com/stevenspatz

- You can get 10% off at BookBaby if you use my link: www.TheCreativePenn.com/bookbaby or just go to BookBaby.com

4.2 Use different formats to create multiple streams of income

However you choose to publish, it's important to consider the various types of products that you can create out of your manuscript. It might be one document on your computer, but you can turn it into different products which provide multiple streams of income.

You can also license these separately, for example, license print rights while retaining ebook and audiobook rights, or retain English language while licensing Worldwide French.

This chapter contains an overview, and you can check out my free ebook, *Successful Self-Publishing: How to Self-Publish and Market Your Book*, for the technical aspects if you want to self-publish. Here are some considerations for the various formats, and remember, you are not your market. So, even if you don't read in a particular format, it's still worth creating.

Ebook

There are lots of ways to read an ebook now, including devices like the Amazon Kindle, Kobo or Tolino readers, but people also read ebooks on Apple Books, Google Play, and other country-specific readers, mobile devices, and apps.

You can self-publish direct to these services and receive 35%-70% royalties depending on the price and territories you choose.

Ebooks can include **hyperlinks** to take the reader directly to your website. You can use this functionality to enhance the reader's experience with video or audio, as well as downloadable extras. You can provide these on a free page or use an email sign-up so you can find out more about the reader and communicate with them further.

Ebooks use **flowable text,** so the design will shift to whatever the device the reader uses. You need to consider this in your ebook design, so the reader has a quality experience. For example, if you have intricate diagrams or tables, these might work well on a tablet but be too small on a mobile device. You could hyperlink to a web page below the diagram so the reader can view a larger image if they want to.

An important aspect of ebook publishing is the **sample**, which a prospective reader will download, read and use to decide whether or not to buy. One of the things that drives me crazy when sampling non-fiction books as a reader is when the entire sample is a Foreword, usually written by someone other than the author. Make sure you get into the book quickly. Use the Foreword in the Front Matter, so it doesn't appear in the sample, or only include it in the print book.

Ebook boxset

An ebook boxset is a single product containing multiple books, representing a great deal for the customer and a higher royalty for you. It should contain at least three books targeted to the same audience and can be by a single author, or you can do a multi-author boxset and split the royalties.

The boxset will need a cover that represents the books inside, and a price that is discounted from buying the multiple books separately.

You can format ebooks and boxsets easily using Vellum. Here's my tutorial:

www.TheCreativePenn.com/format-ebook-print-with-vellum

Paperback

You should definitely do a print version of your book as non-fiction print sells well and is great for live events as well as marketing purposes.

If you have a distribution method in place, for example, if you are a speaker with back of the room sales, or have an offline business, then you might consider doing a print run for your books. Ingram Spark offers volume discounts, or you can use a local printer.

Most independent authors these days use print-on-demand (POD). You upload your cover and interior formatted files to a distributor like Amazon KDP Print, Createspace or Ingram Spark. The books are available for sale on the online stores like Amazon, Barnes and Noble or country-specific sites, as well as in catalogs used by bookstores, universities and libraries.

When a customer orders a book, a single copy is printed and sent directly to them. No up-front costs for printing, no books in your garage, no trips to the post office. No waste, no pulping. It's magic!

Print-on-demand is used by many traditional publishers, as the majority of print books are sold online in the major English-speaking markets of the US, UK, Canada, and Australia.

In choosing the size for your book, check the paperbacks on your bookshelf for the format you prefer. I use 5 x 8 inches for my books, and this works well even for shorter books of 25,000 words. Some US authors like to use a 6 x 9 format, so it will depend on your personal preference and the type of book you're producing.

You will also need to turn your hyperlinks into easily readable text. I use Pretty Links, a Wordpress plug-in that enables you to make easy-to-read URLs. Go through your manuscript and replace any hyperlinks with readable text.

Hardback

You can do print-on-demand hardbacks through IngramSpark, or you can do a custom print run. These are often used for special editions or early print runs. Speaker and entrepreneurial coach Chris Ducker did a special hardback print run for his book, *Rise of the Youpreneur*, saving that edition for his audience. As he described in an interview on The Creative Penn Podcast,

"We printed privately with a company in London for the hardback cover. I was over the moon with it. I couldn't fault it in any way, shape, or form, as a hardcover.

But we decided that we would not make a hardcover version available on Amazon. I'm going to pull that back and hold it for myself and my own live events, and for sending to clients and influencers because the hardcover is a little bit more impressive."

Chris explained how he decided to independently publish for control, but also hired professionals to make the book the best it could be.

Workbooks

Workbook editions are easy to make and provide a surprisingly good additional income, even if you don't do live events. There is an accompanying workbook edition for this book.

Most non-fiction authors include questions and action points, so to create a workbook, just reformat the book into a large edition. You could also add additional questions. For sizing, I use 6 x 9 inches and add lines for people to fill in the answers within the workbook.

Here's my YouTube video on how to turn your book into a workbook:

www.TheCreativePenn.com/workbook

Journals

Some entrepreneurs are now creating journals, which take the idea of the workbook to the next level.

Podcaster at Entrepreneur On Fire, John Lee Dumas, talked about creating *The Mastery Journal* in an interview on The Creative Penn Podcast:

"Physical products cost money to make. There is full leather, silver leaf edges; there are book markers, bands as well as written pages. I hired designers to do this properly."

John used Prouduct.com to source, prototype, then print and ship from China. He used a Kickstarter campaign for the initial run, then Fulfillment by Amazon (FBA) as well as Shopify for ongoing sales. John has built up a large audience through his daily podcast for aspiring entrepreneurs, so he knew he would be able to sell the journals, which is critical if you're going to outlay money to print in advance.

While *The Mastery Journal* is more structured with prompts and exercises to fill in, Joel Friedlander from TheBookDesigner.com created the plain Write Well journal, ideal for writers who want to fill a beautiful journal with their own words with no need for prompts. It has a soft cover, lined pages, a ribbon and a lie-flat spine. In an interview on The Creative Penn Podcast, he explained,

"Journals should be a pleasure to use, and it should lay flat, so you can write in it easily. People carry their journals with them, they stick them in their purse or their briefcase, or even in their pocket, or their backpack. Square corners tend to get banged very easily, they get dog-eared, they fold over. I don't like that. So the solution is the round corner, and that does take special finishing at the printer.

The paper was super important in that it had to be able to absorb all kinds of writing instruments well. You can tell that I'm a minimalist because I created this journal specifically for writers, not for sketch artists, or bullet journal planners, or productivity people. This is just a canvas for writers to write, so it was optimized for that. There's no interruption. It's just lines on the page."

Audiobook

Audiobooks are the most significant growth segment in publishing, and they are a fantastic way to reach non-fiction readers, many of whom increasingly 'read' by listening. Many listeners may buy the book in print format as well, especially if you include bonus content they can only get in the book.

If you want to create audiobooks, you can license your audio rights, or you can use a service to find and work with professional narrators and producers. You can read the book yourself, or you can hire voice talent to narrate for you. Some authors choose to narrate their own book, as I did for *Business for Authors: How to be an Author Entrepreneur.*

I've tried all these options and now choose to hire a professional narrator to read my books and a studio to produce them. Once you find the right voice, it's a repeatable process.

The main site for audiobook production and distribution is ACX.com, which distributes to Audible and iTunes and integrates with the main Amazon stores. ACX have the choice of an exclusive contract for a higher royalty, or a non-exclusive contract where you can also distribute through other services or sell directly from your website.

New opportunities for audiobooks are developing as the market grows. At the time of writing, other services include Findaway Voices and Authors Republic. Kobo has started selling audiobooks, so a service for distribution may emerge there too.

Pricing audio is difficult, since ACX set the price for you based on the length of the book. If you sell direct or use another platform, you can set your own price.

Some authors will offer the audiobook for free as a bonus from the print or ebook, using that to drive email sign-ups.

However you decide to use audio, it's a powerful format that will only continue to grow as voice technology becomes more prevalent with in-home devices like Amazon Echo (Alexa), Google Home and Apple Homepod.

* * *

Those are just some of the formats you could consider for your manuscript, and each provides a new source of income.

Questions:

- What formats will you turn your manuscript into? How will they fit into your business model?

- What do you need to consider for those specific formats?

Resources:

- *Successful Self-Publishing: How to Self-Publish and Market Your Book* – Joanna Penn

- Tutorial on how to format ebooks and print books with Vellum:
www.TheCreativePenn.com/vellum-tutorial

- Find out more on Vellum software:
www.TheCreativePenn.com/vellum

- Interview with Chris Ducker on *Rise of the Youpreneur* which goes into his non-fiction business model and how he produced his books as an independent: www.TheCreativePenn.com/ducker

- Video: How to turn your book into a workbook:
www.TheCreativePenn.com/workbook

- Interview with John Lee Dumas on creating The Mastery Journal:
www.TheCreativePenn.com/johnleedumas

- Interview with Joel Friedlander on creating the Write Well journal:
www.TheCreativePenn.com/writewell

- How to self-publish your own audiobook:
www.TheCreativePenn.com/selfpubaudio

- How to record your own audiobook:
www.TheCreativePenn.com/record-audiobooks-acx

4.3 Non-fiction book covers

People do judge a book by its cover.

Think about your browsing behaviour. You might go to a category, for example, business books, and then the combination of title and cover might make you stop and check the sales description for more clues as to whether you want to read it. This applies whether you're shopping in physical or online stores.

So, your cover is one of the most important marketing aspects for your book.

Research your genre

Every category will have cover conventions to indicate what type of book it is. Compare the fonts on a spirituality book to a business book. Compare the color palette and images used on a memoir to a marketing book.

So the first thing to do is revisit the comparison titles that you have collected and have a look at the cover design for the bestselling titles in that category. Take some screen prints and see if you can identify the key elements of the bestselling books that could work for your book.

Here are some common conventions of non-fiction cover design:

Strong typography

Many non-fiction books use typography as the main design element. This makes it clear at thumbnail size so people shopping on their mobile devices or tablets can easily see the promise to the reader. For example, *High Performance Habits* by Brendon Burchard, *Start with Why* by Simon Sinek, *You are a Badass* by Jen Sincero, or *Why I'm No Longer Talking To White People About Race* by Reni Eddo-Lodge. Some of these books use a brightly colored background to make the book stand out even more.

One clear image

Think about clarity of message and your promise to the reader. Cookbooks and healthy books often do this well, with a gorgeous dish or image, for example, *Genius Foods* by Max Lugavere.

Other examples include economics bestseller *Thinking, Fast and Slow* by Daniel Kahneman, any of Malcolm Gladwell's books, and *Wild* by Cheryl Strayed.

Personal branding with the face of the author or who the book is about

This is relevant for people who are already famous in their niche or who are specifically building a personal brand around themselves.

Examples include *Lean In* by Sheryl Sandberg, *Rich Dad, Poor Dad* by Robert Kiyosaki, *The Universe Has Your Back* by Gabrielle Bernstein or *Rise of the Youpreneur* by Chris Ducker.

This design style also applies to biographies like *Steve Jobs* by Walter Isaacson.

Make sure it's readable at thumbnail size and in black and white

Blurb quotes from other authors are usually too small to make an impact when a reader is shopping on their mobile device. If they use a device like the Kindle Paperwhite reader, as I do, then the shopping experience is in black and white and at thumbnail size.

Consider a different pared-back design for your ebook and audiobook cover and a more detailed print cover where you can add quotes and anything else you want as social proof.

Branding your series

If you're going to write more than one book aimed at the same audience, consider a design format that you can use across them all so that readers instantly recognise your books. A professional cover designer can design a series look and then subsequent books may be cheaper or at least the process will be quicker and easier than designing anew every time.

Use the same font and color palette across your website and your social media to give a consistent impression.

How to find and work with a professional cover designer

Unless you have experience with book cover design, I recommend working with a professional, because they will make your book the best product it can be. You can find a designer through the recommendations of other authors and by checking the Acknowledgments of books you like.

My list of professional book cover designers: www.TheCreativePenn.com/bookcoverdesign

You can also look at book cover design awards, for example, TheBookDesigner.com has awards every month.

Pick a designer who works in your genre and has testimonials from other happy authors. Discuss with them how you're going to work together, price, dates for delivery, and ownership of the final result.

The price you pay for a cover will depend on what you want. Lots of book cover designers have a selection of off-the-shelf covers which will be cheap, or they can design custom covers, so discuss what you need and ask for a quote if appropriate.

You also need to discuss the number of iterations that are allowed in the design process, as it will usually take a few rounds to agree on a final concept. You'll need to give feedback on design options and it's best to be specific rather than just say you don't like something. For example, "I like the typography on option A and the image on option B, but the blue needs to be more like a stormy ocean than a summer sky."

The designer will provide you with files of the appropriate size for self-publishing on the various stores for ebook, print and audiobook. If they don't know what the file sizes should be, then they are not an experienced book cover designer, and you should find someone else to work with.

Finally, pay your designer promptly. You need to be a good client if you want a long-term relationship with any professional, whether it's a graphic designer, book cover designer, or editor. Building up a team of professionals is a key part of being a professional indie author for the long term.

Questions:

- Have you researched the book covers in your niche? What elements are consistent across the bestselling covers that you could possibly use for your book?

- Have you considered consistent branding for your series?

- How will you find a professional book cover designer to work with? How will you ensure the process goes smoothly?

Resources:

- My list of professional book cover designers: www.TheCreativePenn.com/bookcoverdesign

- www.TheBookDesigner.com has cover design awards every month so you can check out other designers

- Video tutorial of the design process: www.TheCreativePenn.com/designtutorial

4.4 Book formatting for non-fiction: Tables, images, graphical elements

Formatting and book design for non-fiction can be complicated, especially if you want to include tables, images, graphics, footnotes and anything else.

Hire a book designer/professional formatter

If you have a budget for your book, consider hiring a professional to do the book design. A designer with experience will know how to handle the various types of layout and will likely use InDesign or another professional program for that purpose. It's easy to spot a book designed by an amateur, so give your book the best chance you can by using a professional.

You can find a list of formatters and free formatting tools here:

www.TheCreativePenn.com/formatting

Do-it-yourself options

If your book is primarily text-based, like this one, or if you're under budgetary constraints, then you can format your book yourself.

I pay a professional book designer for my print books but

I format my own ebooks with Vellum software, which makes formatting fun, and you can more easily control the updates if you do it yourself.

You can also use Scrivener for formatting as well as writing, or use the templates provided by Kindle, Draft2Digital, Reedsy, or other downloadable templates.

Tips for formatting non-fiction

There may be formatting conventions for your genre, e.g. footnotes or citations. Check the Chicago Manual of Style if you want to be exact. Every traditional publisher will have a house style, but if you're going indie, you can use whatever you like.

The key is to **make the layout clear for the reader** using chapter headings, sub-headings, bullet points, indents, call-outs and other formatting options. White space is important to make the book clearer and easy to read.

For print, make everything big enough to be clear. My pet hate is picking up a print book I'm interested in, only to find the font size has been made way too small in order to make the book cheaper to print.

Images, graphics, photos, illustrations

Consider whether you really need these elements in your book, as they will add considerable cost to your print book and also the delivery cost for your ebook, which will reduce your royalties.

Is there a way you could put images and graphical elements

on your website and link to them in the book, or could you remove them altogether?

If you do want to include them, then make sure you have the relevant permissions as per chapter 3.14 and that you have the files in high-resolution format, as this is critical for printing.

Formatting for different editions

You may need to consider different versions of your book for print, ebook and audiobook editions. For example, footnotes and tables work in print, but they don't work well in ebooks as there is no fixed page layout. They also don't work for audiobooks as they can't be read aloud.

In the same way, a beautiful hand-lettered quote in the middle of a print book looks amazing, but it won't work so well in ebook format and will be read aloud in an audio-book, so the design makes no difference. You can't do any visual elements in an audiobook, so referring to tables or images may confuse the listener.

I always start with my ebook format and take that all the way through the editing process. Then I format the ebook version myself in Vellum. Once I'm happy, I output the manuscript to MS Word and update that version with print-specific information like ISBN and change any links to easily readable URLs. For the audiobook version, I remove most of the URLs and add in a link to download the Bibliography and extra information so audiobook listeners can get the extras if they want to.

Questions:

- Does your book have potentially complicated formatting, or is it generally plain text (like this one?)

- Are there formatting conventions you need to take into consideration?

- Will you do your own formatting, use a template, or hire a professional to format your book? What are the pros and cons of your decision?

- Do you have to make any changes for the different formats?

Resources:

- Free formatting options and a list of professionals: www.TheCreativePenn.com/formatting

- Vellum software for formatting ebooks and print: www.TheCreativePenn.com/vellum

- My tutorial on how to format for ebook and print here: www.TheCreativePenn.com/vellum-tutorial

- *The Chicago Manual of Style* – University of Chicago Press

4.5 Pricing your book

"Customers care about price only when they
have nothing else to care about."

Seth Godin

Pricing is most definitely a marketing tool, and if you
self-publish, you have control over your book's price, and
you can change it at any time. If you have a traditional
publisher, then this is not your decision, but you should at
least know the basics so you can understand the merits of
various price points.

Indie authors have an advantage over traditional publishing with ebook pricing, as we can change prices easily and
quickly. Our overheads are lower, and we receive a higher
royalty per sale, so we can afford lower prices. Here are
some other considerations for pricing.

Consider the value to the reader

Readers will pay more for a book that they feel will give
them a tangible return. For example, *How to Pay Off Your
Mortgage with Day Trading* can probably get away with
being priced higher than *How to Get Your Toddler to Eat
Their Greens*.

Value is critically important and will also outweigh page
count. If it's packed with valuable information, non-fiction
readers don't mind a shorter book.

Look at other books in your niche

What price point are books in your genre selling at for print and ebook? For example, if all other ebooks are selling at $7.99, pricing yours at $15.99 won't work.

If all the print books in the niche are at $19.99, pricing too low at $7.99 will also be incorrect. Non-fiction readers are happier to pay higher prices than fiction readers, mainly because they are getting a tangible benefit, and react more to value pricing. They may also buy in multiple formats.

Don't try to match the price of a big-name author's book, as people will always pay more for someone they've heard about.

Make sure you take advantage of comparison pricing as well. For example, even if you think you will sell more ebooks than print, do a print book anyway as it will make the ebook price look better value.

Look at royalty rates by price band

Amazon has specific price bands for royalties, so you need to price between $2.99 and $9.99 if you want a 70% royalty. If you're pricing below or above that, then it's 35%. If you're in KDP Select, it doesn't make so much of a difference, because you'll get paid per page read.

Great on Kindle is a new non-fiction option for 50% royalty, which has no cap on upper pricing and no delivery charge. It's invite-only at the time of writing but may represent a good opportunity for books with a lot of images or books you want to sell at higher prices.

Other stores don't have an upper limit for the higher royalty rate.

For print, decide on profit margin and discounting

The sales price of your print book is calculated from the cost of production + the margin for the print-on-demand company + the profit you add.

I usually add $1.50 - $2 profit per book onto the calculated cost to print. Print pricing is not as flexible as ebook pricing, although you can format the book in different ways to reduce cost.

If you're using discounting through Ingram Spark, ensure you can still make a profit even after discount. I use the lowest discounting possible, with no returns, but then I don't actively market to bookstores. If you want to encourage bookstores to stock your book, then consider a larger discount and allow returns, but that will impact on your profits. It always comes back to your definition of success.

Make sure you adjust global prices by currency

Most of the retail stores have country-specific pricing, and it's well worth setting these individually instead of relying on an automatic exchange rate calculation. For example, if you price at US$4.99 and just leave it to automatically calculate for GBP, then readers in the UK might see £3.21, which is an odd price. It's best to change the UK price to

£2.99 or £3.49, which are prices that readers are more used to seeing.

This is even more important for markets where the exchange rate is more extreme. For example, US$6.99 is equivalent to around 450 Indian rupees (INR). This might be a fair price for a non-fiction ebook in the USA, but if you look at *Outliers* by Malcolm Gladwell on Amazon.in, the price is 165 rupees. If you want to sell in these international markets, then ensure you check prices of comparison titles in those markets.

Using free to sell more books and reach more readers

New authors often have an issue with free books, because they feel that it undervalues the amount of work put in over months or years. But free can be used strategically as a marketing tool and a way to reach readers and make sales in other ways.

Think about the supermarket on a Friday night when they hand out samples of cheese or wine. You taste a little bit for free and then might end up buying a packet of the cheese and a bottle of the wine. It's known as a loss leader in the retail industry, something that gets a new customer in the door and makes a small loss, in order to make a profit with other products.

It's a similar idea with free books.

If you're just starting out, making your book free can help get your book into readers' hands and will result in more reviews. But free works best as a way into your ecosystem if you have other books or products.

Non-fiction authors can use a free ebook as a lead generation tool for courses, membership sites, consulting or affiliate income. My ebook, *Successful Self-Publishing,* is free and people download it every day. It's packed full of useful information on self-publishing, so the customer gets great value, but it also has affiliate links and information about my other books and courses. It also sells a surprising number of print books every month, so it's another revenue stream.

"Don't offer a discount to get someone to buy your book. You offer the discount as part of a marketing plan that should have an impact on your entire business."

Kristine Kathryn Rusch, Discoverability

How do you make your ebook free?

If you're in Amazon KDP Select, you can set your book to free for five days in each 90-day period. All the other sites allow you to set the price to free anytime. If you want to have a perma-free book on Amazon, set your price to free on the other large stores – Kobo, iBooks and Nook – then report the lower price on your Amazon book page. You might have to do this several times, but eventually, Amazon will price-match to free.

Some people consider free to be over-used and claim that people who download books for free often won't read them anyway and are being 'trained' to get free books. There are opinions either way, but if you have no other way of marketing, then a strategic use of free can be a good start.

Price pulsing for promotional sales

Price pulsing is the use of limited-time price changes for a specific sales period. You lower your prices for a short time and promote the sale. Then, you can take advantage of the higher visibility to put your price back up again.

Promotional sales are a normal part of the retail environment. Customers expect to be able to get special deals, and books are no different. If you do a promotional sale, you can expect more downloads of your ebook, exposure to a new audience, higher rankings and even placement on a bestseller list, as well as sell-through to other books, plus exposure for your brand.

It's a good idea to pay for promotion sites around a sale period, for example, use BookBub or Facebook Ads to drive bargain-hunting readers to your book, as covered in chapter 5.3.

You can schedule price changes for Kobo and iBooks, which is great as you can just set and forget, but you have to change them manually for Amazon, Draft2Digital and other sites. Make sure you do this a few days earlier than your sale date, as the price change can take a while to go through, then remember to change it back again later.

Questions:

- What prices are the bestselling books in your niche? Check ebook and print editions for comparison.

- What price will you set for your ebook and your print book?

- Have you checked international market pricing?

- Have you considered free as a marketing tool? Why would it be useful for your book?

Resources:

- *How to Market a Book* – Joanna Penn

- *Discoverability: Help Readers Find You In Today's World of Publishing* – Kristine Kathryn Rusch

4.6 Your book sales description

It's a mammoth task to write a whole book, but it's also a challenge to turn it into a sales description that makes readers want to buy and start reading immediately.

Copywriting is writing text for the purpose of marketing or selling, and it's quite different to writing a book. If you're traditionally published, your publisher will create the sales description for you, but you won't be able to change it. If you're indie, you have to do it yourself (or pay a professional), but you can also change it whenever you like. Most indies change their sales description over time, so just get started, and you can always finesse it later.

Start by revisiting your comparison titles and copy out the book sales description for each. This will give you a sense of the language used and how the description is structured. It's not a summary of the book. It's an advert that will hopefully make the reader want to buy.

What problem will your book solve for the reader? What question does it answer?

The goal of a non-fiction book is usually to solve a particular problem. The reader is searching for answers, and they need to know that your book addresses them specifically. It has to be worth buying.

You could use a question at the top of the sales description.

For *How to Market a Book*, the first line is "Do you want to sell more books and reach more readers?"

The same applies to any genre. It's all about empathy with your reader. What problem do *they* have? What language do *they* resonate with?

For example, I talked to a clinical psychologist whose a book on cognitive behavioral therapy (CBT) wasn't selling. His sales description was overly technical about the therapy itself, whereas readers would more likely be searching for help with their problem. His hook could be "Do you need help with depression or anxiety?" rather than "Do you need CBT?"

Establish why you are the person to help

Once you've identified the problem, you can write about why you're the person to help and establish your expertise. The reader needs to know that they can trust you to help.

Bryan Cohen, author of *How to Write a Sizzling Synopsis*, explained this in an interview on The Creative Penn Podcast.

"Something that non-fiction authors need to do that they aren't doing is to establish their own expertise in the book description. People often don't like to sell themselves. But they sell themselves short when they don't mention why they are the person to help.

The reader needs to know that not only does this book solve the problem, but that you're the person who is going to solve their problem and that they can trust you."

Should you use a table of contents?

You can include a table of contents, or condense the various parts with mini-headlines that entice the reader. You can also use bullet-point formatting, which makes it easier to read.

The phrasing here is important, for example, use "In this book, you will discover," rather than "In this book, I will teach." The word 'you' is incredibly important in copywriting and keeps the focus on the reader, because they are thinking, "What's in it for me?"

Blurbs from other authors and media

One study by BookBub found that a quote from a well-known author boosted click-through rate by 22%. A quote from an author like Stephen King will get a better click-through than a quote from a publication like *Publishers Weekly*. So quotes from well-known authors are great if you can get them. But most of us won't get a cover quote from the biggest names in our genre.

If you have quotes from other authors, publications or blogs, put them in the editorial review section, which you can access through Amazon Author Central.

Formatting and testing

You can format your sales description with basic HTML for the online stores, which will give you larger headlines, sub-heads and bullets. You can use Author Central to do this, hand-code it yourself, or I use Author Marketing Club's Enhanced Description Maker, part of their premium service.

You can test different changes to your sales description over time, and even if you don't want to do that, make a note in your calendar to review your sales description every six months, or at least annually. Life moves on, you change, and you will likely want to update it over time.

Questions:

- What problem will your book solve for your reader? What question does it answer?

- Why are you the right person to help? How can you establish your expertise or experience?

- Have you identified bestselling books in your genre and copied out the sales description, so you have something to model?

- Have you written a draft of your sales description? It's a good idea to start early and work on it as you write.

- If you have already published books, are there ways you could improve your existing sales description?

Resources:

- Interview with Bryan Cohen, author of *How to Write a Sizzling Synopsis*, on The Creative Penn Podcast: www.TheCreativePenn.com/bryancohen

- Amazon Author Central for the US store: author-central.amazon.com Also available for the UK and other country stores.

- Author Marketing Club's Enhanced Description Maker, part of their premium service: www.TheCreativePenn.com/amc

4.7 Categories and keywords

Metadata is the information that the book sales sites use to categorize your book, and they use it in the algorithms to help with book recommendations. It's important for making sure that readers can find your book and includes:

- Title and sub-title

- Series title

- Sales description

- Categories

- Keywords

Categories and keywords in particular are important in terms of your book being discovered. As 'big data' becomes more prevalent in our society, it's likely that even the text of your book will eventually be used as metadata. Again, being indie is an advantage, as we can change these fields over time and react to changes in the market.

Categories

Categories are used on all online sales platforms and you can choose between two and five in general. The aim is to be granular enough that your book can stand out but not so deep down the hierarchy that no one ever shops there.

For example, there's absolutely no point in putting your work in a top level category like Business & Money, as people just won't be able to find it among the mega-bestsellers. Readers tend to shop in sub-categories, so this is where you need to put your book. Focus on the more granular categories e.g. Business & Money/Personal Finance/Retirement Planning. Go to Amazon and drill down into the categories until you can't go any deeper.

Go back to your comparison titles and check which category they are in. Go to the book page on Amazon, scroll down and you'll find the categories the book is listed in and ranks for.

If you self-publish, you choose categories in the publishing process. You can also target 'browse categories' through keywords on Amazon. For example, you can get into the sub-category of Business & Money/Entrepreneurship & Small Business/Startups by using the keyword 'startup' when you publish the book.

If you need help deciding on sub-categories to target on Amazon, check out the reports on K-lytics, which go into detail on specific genres so you can work out how best to position your book.

Keywords

Keywords, or keyword phrases, are a separate metadata field on the publishing platforms, and you can usually select seven.

Use the Amazon search bar to discover the words and phrases that people are searching for. Just start typing in the box and you will get a dropdown that auto-populates based on the most popular searches. Spend some time trying different combinations and you'll be amazed at what you find.

The principle is the same for fiction and non-fiction, but for non-fiction, it's even better because you can title your book to match the keywords that people search for.

My first book was originally called *How To Love Your Job or Find a New One*. After discovering keywords, I changed the title to *Career Change*. The book began to sell more, since people were searching for the keyword phrase 'career change' on Amazon, whereas they weren't searching for the original title.

For more help, check out KDP Rocket, which generates keywords for specific search terms.

Questions:

- What is metadata and why is it important for your book?

- What categories are your comparison titles using?

- What 3-5 categories are most appropriate for your book?

- What keywords might you use for your book?

Resources:

- K-lytics for niche and category research:
  www.TheCreativePenn.com/genre

- KDP Rocket for keyword and category research:
  www.TheCreativePenn.com/rocket

4.8 Turn your non-fiction book into a multi-media course

People want to learn and increasingly, education is moving online.

Why create an online course from your book?

You can **reach new customers**. Some people don't want to read, preferring to consume and learn by video and audio.

You can **reach a global audience** with online training, whereas live events will always be restricted to those who can attend in person.

It provides an **additional revenue stream** from the same basic material, as you can charge more for multimedia information and a community (if you provide it).

You can **integrate the course into your marketing funnel**, so the book can lead into the course, which in turn can lead to other income streams like speaking, consulting or coaching, as described in chapter 2.2 on business models.

Check out my multi-media course based on this book:

www.TheCreativePenn.com/writenonfiction

Decide on the topic and title for the course

You might decide to use exactly the same name, branding and table of contents for your course as you did for your book. Or you could decide on something more tangential.

For example, you might have a single multi-media course on Knitting for Beginners: Basic Stitches and Designs. Then you might have 10 different books on knitting different designs that lead to the same course. You could also do the reverse with one book and multiple smaller courses.

It's important to note up front that you don't need to do a mega-course that takes months to build, costs thousands of dollars to make and buy, and launches with a fanfare. That used to be the primary model but now online courses are so widely available, the modular approach is more common. So you can create a mini-course on how to knit a woollen scarf and sell it for $49 and be up and running in no time!

Plan the contents

Once you have the topic and title, you need to break down your table of contents. I use Scrivener to plan my courses in the same way as I do for my books.

This should include the videos you need to create as well as any extra material, for example, workbooks, tutorials, bonus interviews, checklists, templates, and other downloads. The course needs to be great value, so this is your chance to deliver above expectations.

One tip when planning your material is to consider anything that might age or become obsolete over time. Try to keep those elements in separate videos so you can easily find them and re-record an updated version when you need to. For example, if you're teaching technical software like WordPress or Facebook, the user interface will change periodically so you'll need to re-record, whereas evergreen content on marketing principles won't need to be re-recorded.

You also need to consider whether to include a live element or community aspect to your course. This might be live webinars, Q&A sessions, online office hours, or a private Facebook community or forum. Whether you do this will depend on how you want to use your time and your pricing levels.

Decide on your course hosting and sales technology

You can build a custom site for your course, using WordPress themes or designs that incorporate shopping carts like Woocommerce.

Personally, I prefer to focus on content, not technology, so I use and recommend Teachable for my course solution. It's scalable, so you can pay as you go. It adapts per platform and you don't have to worry about hosting, as it's all covered and supported. They can manage payments and affiliates for you, or you can connect a payment gateway of your own if you're expecting higher volumes. They also include email functionality and ways to hook into other platforms.

Whatever set-up you choose, you will definitely need PayPal, so if you don't have a business account there already, start the set-up early as you'll need to go through anti-money-laundering checks before it's fully functional. PayPal also throttle payments you can send and receive if you're a new user, so you need to ramp up slowly.

Plan your time

It always takes longer than you think to write a book or build a course, so plan some extra time in your schedule.

Even if you've written the book, it still takes time to adapt the material to a course format. You might also want to conduct bonus interviews, or create extra material.

If you want to record a 20 minute video, you'll need to prepare the content, set up your equipment, record the video with the inevitable re-takes, edit the video and upload it to the hosting site. It will likely take 2-4 hours to complete this 20 minute video, especially if this is a new skill for you.

Create the content

You may have to learn new skills, but once you do, creating videos and audios can become an important part of your business. I have certainly found it a major part of my creative business.

I use Screenflow on the Mac for recording screen-capture video, or you can use Camtasia on the PC. For direct to camera filming, you can use your smartphone or webcam for starters, or do some investigation into better cameras if you have the budget – but it's certainly not essential.

Use Audacity for audio recording, or I use Amadeus Pro on the Mac. A good microphone can help with sound quality. I use the Blue Yeti.

Once you have the technical stuff set up, then it's more about practice and presentation skills, especially for video. If you've done any public speaking before, you'll know that energy and delivery style are important for an engaging presentation. I find making videos tiring, so I schedule separate recording batches and editing time.

Remember to back up all your material, in case of technical glitches.

Create your sales page

Just as writing a book can be easier than writing the sales description, creating a course can be easier than writing the sales page! The best idea is to model other courses in your niche, noting the language used and the different aspects they cover on the sales page.

Include the transformation for the buyer, as well as detailed benefits, plus how the course is set up and any extras. If you have testimonials from happy customers, these are a great addition and you can always add them over time. Use images to bring your sales page alive.

You could also make a sales video explaining the benefits of the course and why you're the right person to teach it. This also gives people a taste of your presenting style.

When pricing your course, consider the other options in your niche, as well as how much of a fan base you already have and how much value you're providing. Don't price too low, especially if you're including any kind of live component that will take more of your time.

Consider working with affiliates

Affiliate relationships are mutually beneficial in that you get extra sales and new people into your audience, the customer gets a great course, and the affiliate will get a percentage of sale – usually 40-50% for online courses.

If you want to work with affiliates, you need to have an effective sales process and proven conversion, as well as tested webinars and bonus materials. I'm an affiliate for a number of courses and only work with partners with happy customers and provide value for my time in promoting the product.

Many of the course platforms have an affiliate program as part of their service.

Launch your course

Once your course is ready, you can launch!

Your launch process will depend on how big your existing audience is, your personality type, and also whether you're doing an evergreen course (always for sale) or one that only opens periodically.

Options for marketing your course include:

- A series of free videos and other content available for email sign-up that lead into a buy sequence

- A live webinar with teaching followed by a pitch

- An evergreen email sequence that leads to a sales page

- Blog posts, podcasts, content marketing and social media, in the same way as you would promote your book or other products/services

Questions:

- Why would you consider turning your book into an online course? What are the benefits and what are the downsides?

- What will your course cover? Will it mirror your book, or be a sub-set, or encompass a much wider topic?

- What will your course be called?

- What will the content of the course be?

- Have you researched and decided on the technical solution?

- Have you planned your time for creating the content?

- Have you looked at examples of sales pages in your niche and considered how yours might work?

- What price will you sell your course at?

- How will you launch and market your course?

- What are your next steps toward creating an online course?

Resources:

- Teachable is my recommended course hosting platform: www.TheCreativePenn.com/teachable

- Screenflow for Mac: www.telestream.net/screenflow

- Camtasia for PC: www.techsmith.com/video-editor.html

- Blue Yeti microphone: www.TheCreativePenn.com/blueyeti

- Skype for recording interviews: www.Skype.com

- ECamm Call Recorder for Skype (Mac): www.ecamm.com/mac/callrecorder/

- Pamela call recorder for PC: www.pamela.biz

- Audacity audio software: www.audacityteam.org

- How to Write Non-Fiction Multimedia Course: www.TheCreativePenn.com/writenonfiction

* * *

For more detail on how to build an online course, check out the free *Course Creation Toolkit Bundle* by Joseph Michael, the Scrivener Coach, who has made multi-six-figures from his Learn Scrivener Fast course:

www.TheCreativePenn.com/coursecreation

4.9 Updating your books over time

Books are incredible. They can make you money during your lifetime and up to 70 years after you die, which is the term of copyright. But of course, that only works if you nurture the book over time.

Here are some ways that you can keep your book alive for the long term.

(1) Update the contents in a new edition

If you self-publish, it's easy to update your book files. Most of us do this at least once a year to update back matter, links and any out-of-date information, as well as fix typos.

Minor changes don't warrant a new edition, so you can just change your source files and upload the new version for both ebook and print. You can use the same ISBN, and you'll retain your reviews. For more help on the technical aspects, see my book, *Successful Self-Publishing*.

However, if you want to make major changes, as I did when I republished *Career Change* with new chapters and a new focus, then the book will need to be a new edition. You'll need to use a new ISBN for your print edition, and it's recommended to publish a new ebook edition. You will lose your reviews, but on the flip side, you will make new sales. I did this for the Third Edition of *How to Market a Book* as it was significantly different enough to warrant a new edition.

(2) Update the cover

Book cover design trends change over time, and covers can look dated after a few years, which will eventually drive down sales. You might also decide that your cover doesn't adequately represent your book and you want to change it to try and boost sales.

You can change a cover easily if you self-publish. Upload a new cover file to the ebook and print retailers. You don't need a new ISBN or edition for a new cover. If you have a traditional publisher, you could always request a cover change or look at getting your rights back if they are not keeping the book up to date.

(3) Change the title

Sometimes a book just has the wrong title. Seth Godin, bestselling author of multiple marketing books, admits that he got the title wrong to his book, *All Marketers Are Liars*.

"The irony is that I did a lousy job of telling a story about this book. The original cover seemed to be about lying and seemed to imply that my readers (marketers) were bad people. For people who bothered to read the book, they could see that this wasn't true, but by the time they opened the cover, it was too late. A story was already told. I had failed."

The book was re-titled and re-covered a number of years after publication as *All Marketers Tell Stories*, with the cover showing the words *Are Liars* crossed out as a nod to the original.

I did the same with my first non-fiction book, *How to Enjoy Your Job or Find A New One*. After I discovered the principles of Search Engine Optimization, it became clear that *Career Change* would be a more appropriate title, especially as I did end up changing my career by putting the principles outlined in the book into place.

The requirement for a new edition is more about the interior contents, so you can still use the same ISBN, but make sure you include the words 'Previously published as' in the book and also on your sales description.

Some authors worry about readers being confused and perhaps accidentally buying the same book twice. But let's be honest, most of us don't sell gazillions of copies, so the chances are small, especially if you're changing titles in order to sell more books. So don't worry about it, just do the best for your book's chances of being found and read!

Questions:

- Why might you need to update your book in years to come?

- How could you prepare for this so it is easier to change later on?

Resources:

- *Successful Self-Publishing: How to Self-Publish and Market Your Book* – Joanna Penn

- Seth Godin's article on updating *All Marketers are Liars*: http://sethgodin.typepad.com/all_marketers_are_liars/2009/11/a-new-cover-a-new-foreword-but-the-same-book.html

Part 5: Marketing Non-Fiction

5.1 Two models of marketing and the importance of mindset

"Everything you and your business does is marketing."

James Watt, *Business for Punks*

This book is about *writing* non-fiction, but the journey doesn't end when you have a finished book in the world. I learned this the hard way after I wrote and published my first book, *Career Change.* The books didn't sell because no one knew they existed, and so I started my journey into learning about book marketing.

This section is just a taster on marketing, and of course, you can dive down deeper on every single one of these topics. You can find more detail on book marketing in *How to Market a Book,* available in ebook, print and audiobook editions.

The two models of marketing

In my experience, non-fiction is much easier to market than fiction, because readers are specifically interested in a topic or they want an answer to a question. It's also easier to attract an audience before you even have a book, as you can educate, entertain or inspire by other means. But of course, it still takes effort to sell books, and in the writer's life, marketing often takes as long as writing.

There are two main models of marketing for non-fiction that relate directly to the business models covered in chapter 2.2.

Book-centered marketing relies on producing multiple books in a popular genre targeting the same audience and using paid ads to drive traffic directly to the book sales page. It is usually part of the high-production business model.

Author-centered marketing is about building a personal brand and attracting your target market over time through content marketing, speaking, social media, and paid advertising.

In this model, the non-fiction author will also have other parts to their business, either in person as a speaker, consultant, coach or other practitioner, or online with multimedia courses and affiliate marketing. These authors and business-owners are already engaged in various forms of marketing, which can easily be extended into book promotion.

Of course, you can use both methods at the same time, as I do. They just work in different ways. The next few chapters will go into these models in more detail, but before we go any further, it's time to reframe marketing so that you can successfully sell your books.

The marketing mindset

Let's face it. We'd all love someone else to handle the marketing. But times have changed, and at some point, you will have to get involved in selling your book however you choose to publish.

You are responsible for your own success.

Marketing will be a lot easier and more fun if you start by changing your mindset. Here are some ways to reframe book marketing so that you can read the rest of this section with a new perspective.

Marketing is sharing what you love with people who will appreciate hearing about it.

It's not tweeting 'buy my book' repeatedly or accosting innocent readers in bookstores. It's connecting with people around the topic you're passionate about and being useful, entertaining or inspirational along the way.

Marketing is creative.

If you consider it as an inherent part of the process, rather than something separate, you will enjoy it more. For example, if you're doing some research, share pictures of the trip, whether they're relevant to your book or not. Give an insight into your world.

Marketing is a learnable skill.

You don't need a degree in marketing to sell books, but you do need to learn new things, try them out and practice over time. You can hire other people to help you, but if you upskill yourself, it will be cheaper, more effective (since no one knows your book as well as you do), and more authentic. You might even enjoy it!

Choose the specific type of marketing you want to do based on your personality.

For example, I'm an introvert (INFJ on the Myers-Briggs) and prefer online marketing like podcasts or blog posts over in-person events and networking, which may be suitable for more extroverted writers.

Marketing is more than a book launch, especially if you want to make a consistent living with your writing.

You can continue to sell books, products, and services for years to come if you integrate marketing into your creative and production processes. Let's get into the details.

Questions:

- What are the two models of marketing?
- How can you embrace the marketing mindset?

Resources:

- *How to Market a Book* – Joanna Penn

5.2 Book-centered marketing

"Creating more work is one of the most effective marketing techniques of all."

Ryan Holiday, Perennial Seller

The great news is that books themselves can be marketing, and your writing can be the method you use to attract readers. You don't need social media, or blogging, or media interviews or anything but your words on the page, if that's what you prefer.

However, this approach does rely on having a lot of books so that you can use them for marketing purposes as well as producing on a regular schedule. It suits the more prolific writer or the author who has already built a backlist.

(1) Write books that people want to read and make them easy to find

The easiest way to market a non-fiction book is to write books that people want in the first place. We went through these basics in Part 2, but if you're struggling with marketing, then revisit these questions to ensure your book is positioned well.

- Research the categories and sub-categories for your target market

- Use a keyword-specific book title and/or sub-title

- Use a professional cover that resonates with your genre

- Use an effective book sales description that catches the attention of your target readers and makes them want to buy

- Make sure the sample of your book entices them to read more or buy now

(2) Write more non-fiction books and vary the length

If you have more books, you have more ways for people to discover you and more streams of income, so the number of ways to sell and market grows exponentially.

Remember, you don't have to write huge books every time. A lot of non-fiction books are quite short, around 25,000-40,000 words, so you don't have to spend years writing one book. Try writing several shorter ones instead.

If you write more books in the same genre, readers might buy more than one, so you can make more income per customer.

(3) Write in a series

If you write multiple books aimed at the same audience around the same topics, you can use the Series field on the publishing platforms to link them together. This gives the reader a cue that there are more books they might be interested in, and sometimes you will get a series page that links the books together.

(4) Use a free book to attract people into your ecosystem

My ebook, *Successful Self-Publishing*, is free on all the major stores and writers interested in getting their books out into the world download it every day.

When a reader downloads the book, it signals to the retailer's algorithm that this reader might be interested in my other books, and many of those who download the free book go on to buy other books – or even that same book in print format.

It includes links to my courses, podcast and YouTube channel, as well as more resources, tutorials, affiliate links and other products and services the reader might find useful. Plus, it links to my email sign-up offer for the Author 2.0 Blueprint, which brings people further into my ecosystem. This is useful for them, and over time, profitable for me. All from a free ebook!

You can do something similar in your niche. Provide a free, high-quality book packed full of useful information, inspiration or entertainment and put it on the major ebook stores with a keyword-rich title as another way into your business ecosystem.

(5) Create ebook box-sets

If you want to create multiple streams of income, an ebook boxset can be a great way to add more revenue without writing more books. You need to have at least three books targeted to the same niche and then create one file with those books in them. Publish them with a new cover and at a discounted price to buying them separately.

You can publish these for a short-term promotion, or for longer-term income. I'd recommend using evergreen books, rather than those you need to update a lot, since the maintenance of files over time can become unwieldy otherwise.

Those are just some ideas for book-centered marketing, where the book itself becomes your main marketing collateral, and they can work alongside other forms of marketing.

Questions:

- What are some ways that you could do book-centered marketing?

Resources:

- *Perennial Seller: The Art of Making and Marketing Work that Lasts* – Ryan Holiday

- *Write to Market: Deliver a Book That Sells* – Chris Fox

5.3 Paid advertising for non-fiction books

"Good marketers realize marketing is not an expense, but an investment."

Seth Godin

If you have a budget for book marketing, you can use paid advertising to reach readers, sell more books, and build your email list.

Your sales may drop off unless you sustain advertising over time, so this strategy should be used in conjunction with other marketing techniques. You can use paid advertising if you're starting out, so you don't need to have spent years building an author platform to use it.

I use paid advertising as a key part of my non-fiction marketing. These are just a few of the possible options for paid advertising to get you started.

Email list services

Paid promotional sites have built email lists of avid readers who might be interested in your book. If you're combining an email blast with a short-term promotional price drop, you can spike your sales.

Note: This is NOT the same as 'buying email lists.' Don't do that! With reputable services, you won't be given the email list, but your book will be sent out to those readers for you.

You can use email list services like BookBub Featured Deals, FreeBooksy, BargainBooksy and others. These focus on specific target genres and generally have fewer options for non-fiction promotion than they do for fiction. At the time of writing, BookBub Featured Deals include Business as a category, but with nothing more specific, e.g. Finance or Self-Help, both of which are huge in the non-fiction market.

If your book doesn't easily fit into an available niche, you can use more granular paid advertising options through Facebook, Amazon Ads, and BookBub Ads as covered below.

Amazon Ads

If you're new to paid ads, Amazon Ads are a great way to start. There are fewer choices, they are technically simpler, and you won't accidentally break the bank. You can spend a few dollars and build up your confidence before trying other platforms.

You have to be the publisher of your book to use some forms of Amazon Ads, so they can't be used by traditionally published authors or those that have used an intermediary service to publish.

Login at ams.amazon.com with your usual address and you will see your books available to advertise on the US store. There are also ad platforms for some of the other stores, e.g. UK or Canada, but the functionality is different and not as integrated with the KDP Dashboard.

Check examples of ads by going to popular books in your genre. Underneath the 'Customers who bought this item also bought' area is another line of books marked 'Sponsored products related to this item.' You may also see a single book advertised under the buy button or a headline banner for some search terms. Advertising options will change over time, so check the help documentation for more details.

Amazon Ads are great because the image is always your book cover, so you have one less thing to think about. You just have to come up with the advertising text and the audience targeting, which can be keywords you choose or auto-targeted. I use KDP Rocket to find keywords to use with each book.

You can do this manually by using the Search bar dropdown, but Rocket helps you go much faster, saving time and energy. Then you can set up AMS ads with those keywords.

I've found that auto-targeting only works well with books that have an easily recognizable audience. It has worked for my non-fiction as there is a sub-niche of people who buy writing-related books and the algorithm can clearly group them under my non-fiction author name, Joanna Penn. If you have published lots of different books under the same author name, auto-targeting probably won't be so effective.

Amazon Ads give you an ACoS (Advertising Cost of Sales) score that enables you to quickly see whether the ad is providing a positive return-on-investment. If it's under 70%, then the ad should be making you money, but at the time of writing, the reports are known to be inaccurate as the ACoS score only relates to actual purchases and doesn't incorporate print books, audiobooks or Kindle Unlimited (KU) borrows. It also doesn't take into account read-through to other books, or the other potential revenue streams you can make from a free book through affiliate or product sales.

So it's best to have some idea of your baseline sales and see if your ads raise that baseline over time. It's a basic guideline, but if you're not into detailed data analysis, it's better than nothing.

BookBub Ads

These ads are separate to BookBub Featured Deals. You set up an ad and can then target readers in a category or readers of a certain author at any time. This can be effective for non-fiction, as you can target the readers of authors writing in the same niche and it will include the names of indie authors as well as traditionally published authors, unlike Facebook Ads which often just have the latter.

Go to partners.bookbub.com to get started.

Facebook Ads

Facebook Ads can be as granular as you like, selecting a target audience by demographics including location, gender and age, as well as interests, e.g. Martial Arts or Travel Photography. You can also select TV shows, films, magazines, well-known authors and behavior like mobile usage.

If you have an email list, you can load the data and Facebook will create an audience from that list (while adhering to data protection laws with encryption). You can create a LookaLike audience from that list, extrapolating out to find more people with similar interests in a chosen population.

If you use videos on your Facebook page, you can use engagement with those videos as a way to build an audience, as well as traffic to your website if you put the Facebook Pixel on your site. Make sure you have a Privacy Policy in place if you want to use this option.

I mainly use Facebook Ads for higher revenue opportunities like webinars and courses, but I will also boost content that tangentially relates to my books, for example, a video on self-doubt that ties into my book, *The Successful Author Mindset*.

There are plenty of books on the detail of how to use these paid advertising platforms, but as the technology changes regularly, make sure the edition is up to date.

Kobo Writing Life Promotions

If you are not exclusive on Amazon, and you publish direct to Kobo Writing Life, you can get access to the Promotions tab by contacting the KWL team. You can submit your books to different promotions every month with both paid and free options.

You won't always get the promotions you apply for, but when you do, it can make a big difference to sales on Kobo in various territories, and they do have specific options for non-fiction authors.

Buy ads on targeted media like podcasts or blogs

There are hundreds of podcasts in every niche these days, and thousands of blogs. Many of these have paid advertising opportunities so you can reach a targeted audience.

Some authors will look at paid ads in print newspapers and magazines. That can still be effective but is far more difficult to measure than digital methods, where clicks and sales are more easily tracked.

How to evaluate advertising opportunities

There are plenty of paid advertising options out there with more opportunities every day, but you have to look at some metrics to decide on whether to invest. Here are some criteria to consider:

- How targeted is the opportunity for your niche audience? For example, there's no point advertising a finance book on a vegan cooking blog.

- How much traffic does the site get, or how many downloads does the podcast get per week? Is it worth the money? Most sites with advertising will state how much traffic they have as well as rates for advertising.

- Can you get personal recommendations from other authors who have had success this way?

Questions:

- Do you have a budget for paid advertising? (If not, consider other options like free content marketing)

- What are some of the advertising services that you could consider?

- How will you evaluate advertising opportunities?

- What are your next steps around paid advertising?

Resources:

- Amazon Marketing Services for the US Amazon store: www.TheCreativePenn.com/rocket

- BookBub Featured Deals and Ads: partners. bookbub.com

- Go direct to Kobo Writing Life and request access to the Promotions tab: www.Kobo.com/writinglife

- *Help! My Facebook Ads Suck: Simple Steps to Turn Those Ads Around* – Michael Cooper

- *Mastering Amazon Ads: An Author's Guide* – Brian D. Meeks

* * *

If you'd like a comprehensive course, I recommend Mark Dawson's *Advertising for Authors*.

You can sign up for the waitlist at: www.TheCreativePenn.com/ads

5.4 Author-centered marketing. The power of a personal brand

"A personal brand business is the last pivot
you'll ever need to make."

Chris Ducker, Rise of the Youpreneur

The author-centered marketing approach suits non-fiction authors really well, especially if you develop an ecosystem and business model that ties all your income streams together. This concept is the basis of my own business. The compounding effect of a personal brand means that it keeps growing over time, independent of the vagaries of an algorithm or paid ads to sell books, products and services.

Why you need a personal brand

It's the best time in history to be an author. You can write and publish whatever you like. You can reach people globally from your laptop and make a living from your writing.

But we also live an increasingly competitive marketplace where everyone is an author, every niche feels saturated, and new voices add to the noise every day. Artificial Intelligence (AI) tools have started to write newspaper articles and read our podcasts and audio through in-home devices. It won't be long until they are also writing the books that fill our stores.

The only way to stand out is by being you.

Tell your story, share your face, your voice, your smile. Be authentic and show the world that you are a real human. In a world with so many fake brands, people want to connect with people, and do business with those they know, like and trust.

There will always be someone cheaper than you, faster than you – but no one else can be you.

This does not mean making up a story or a brand to fit the book (or product or course or whatever) you want to sell. It means being honest about who you are and what you want to create.

Who are you?

"The one thing that you have that nobody else has is you. Your voice, your mind, your story, your vision."

Neil Gaiman

This is not your LinkedIn bio. This is looking at yourself on a deeper level. It means figuring out what your brand might look like, what you want to share and what aspects of you might connect with other people, as well as what is sustainable for you. Here are some questions to consider:

- What are the things that stand out in your memory as key parts of your life?

- What are some of your failures as well as your successes?

- What words would you use to define yourself? How would other people describe you?

- What do you enjoy? What are you attracted to? Consider books, movies, images, colors, games, places, events, sports, food – really think about it. Every single one of the things you're interested in is a niche where other people are, too.

- What kind of personality are you? Maybe try a few personality tests to help you work this out. I like the Myers-Briggs (I'm INFJ), but they all enable us to catch a glimpse of a facet of ourselves.

- What are your values? For example, my number one value is freedom, and it shapes my life choices and business decisions as well as my marketing.

Sustainable for the long term

Don't worry. You don't have to launch your book as a fully-formed personal brand.

You can just be you and learn along the way. If you share your journey authentically, your brand is something unique to you that grows and changes as you do.

Create meaningful work that is consistent with your values, and people will be attracted to you because of what you put out into the world. They will be happy to support you because people love to support creators who share their story and resonate with the same values.

Don't fake anything. It's exhausting and unnecessary. Just be you and share what matters to you and this can become a sustainable basis to your business for the long-term.

I know this works because it's how I built my own business, The Creative Penn Limited, over the last ten years as I shared my journey from first book to making a multi-six-figure income as a writer. Perhaps you bought this book because you listen to my podcast, or watch my videos on YouTube, or read my blog, or follow me on social media. Let's face it, there are lots of books on writing non-fiction. Why did you buy mine?

If you didn't know me before, since you've made it this far through the book, you know more about me now. Perhaps you'll be interested in checking out my other books or listening to the podcast or audiobooks. Because you will have heard my voice and my story, and (hopefully) it resonated in some way.

Setting boundaries. A curated version of you.

There are some people who seem to share everything online – and I mean everything. But don't worry, you can set your boundaries and still have a genuine personal brand.

I share aspects of my life around writing or the research topics around my fiction. I share pictures from my trips on social media and my weekly creative musings on the podcast. But I rarely share pictures of my husband, and I keep my family private.

I also curate my feelings on the rollercoaster of the creative life. Everyone has difficult days, but I don't go online and moan or weep or rage. That stays within my private space as I choose to be a positive voice. I've shared my fears and anxieties in order to help others in *The Successful Author Mindset*, but if I'm having a bad day, there's no need to share it every time.

So set your boundaries, and then share honestly within them.

> "Authenticity is a collection of choices that we have to make every day. It's about the choice to show up and be real. The choice to be honest. The choice to let our true selves be seen."
>
> *Brené Brown, The Gifts of Imperfection*

Marketing around a personal brand

If you embrace the idea of you as the brand, then everything becomes part of your marketing efforts. Everything can be a way to reach readers, including:

- Content marketing like blogging, podcasting, video

- Social media and image sharing

- PR and traditional media like radio and TV

- Speaking at live events

- Networking events, trade shows, specialist industry meetings

Anything where you are present either physically or virtually can be a way to attract people to your books, products and services. It's also the most sustainable form of marketing as you will be you for the long term.

Questions:

- Why is a personal brand so important?

- What are some of the aspects that could make up your personal brand? What are some of your key memories, successes and failures?

- What do you enjoy? What niches are you already interested or involved in?

- What kind of personality are you?

- What are your values and how do they relate to what you want to build?

- How can you make this sustainable for the long term?

- How will you define your boundaries and still share authentically?

Resources:

- *Rise of the Youpreneur: The Definitive Guide to Becoming the Go-To Leader in Your Industry and Building a Future-Proof Business* – Chris Ducker

- *The Gifts of Imperfection: Let Go Of Who You Think You're Supposed To Be And Embrace Who You Are* – Brené Brown

- *The Successful Author Mindset: A Handbook for Surviving the Writer's Journey* – Joanna Penn

5.5 Build your author website

Regardless of how you publish or market, you need a home on the Internet, somewhere to point people to from the various social media sites, a hub for all the links to your books, products and events over time. It might also host your blog, podcast or videos.

Writing is a long-term career, and if you want to take it seriously as a business, you should own and control your website, because only then can you guarantee the longevity and security of the site over time.

Some authors build their author hub with a Facebook page or other social media site. But remember Myspace. The popularity of these websites shift over time, and they also change the rules. If you use a free site or free hosting, you do not own the site or the content, and the company could go under or turn off that service at any point. Everything you've built may disappear unless you own, control and back up your site.

Of course, you can start with a free site, but be sure to back it up and consider shifting to paid hosting as your author career develops.

Your domain name and website set-up

Many first-time authors make the mistake of setting up a site around their book title or theme, without considering a longer-term career. I did this with my first book and soon left that site behind as I moved into writing about other subjects.

It's best to buy the URL for your author name if you can, or use an initial or the word 'author' after your name if that is already taken. If you use multiple brands, you can buy other URLs and redirect them to the same site at first and build separate ones over time if you want.

This is not a technical book, so if you want the details, check out my tutorial on **how to build your author website** in under 30 minutes:

www.TheCreativePenn.com/authorwebsite

I take you through how to set up a basic author website without spending much money, and it includes the various sites I use for hosting and design. It's a good idea to keep it simple and learn the basics yourself so that you can change your design and content over time as you learn more skills.

Many premium WordPress themes have SEO design, making it easy for search engines to find and index your site, as well as mobile-responsive frameworks so readers can use your site on whatever device they prefer.

Don't obsess over design until you have more of a clue about what you want to do with your author brand.

My sites are almost unrecognizable since their first iterations, but the beauty of WordPress is that you can change the design and make it mobile-compatible while still retaining the underlying content. Build your site with a clean, easy-to-read and simple design and update later.

Here's my tutorial on how to set up the Author Pro Word-Press Theme:

www.TheCreativePenn.com/setup-author-pro-theme

We all start with nothing

No traffic to our site.

No sales.

No followers.

No email list.

That's just the way it is. Building a career as a professional writer is a long-term project, so don't worry if you have nothing right now. It will grow over time, as will your profile as a writer if you keep building it consistently. I would be nowhere if I hadn't started with a terrible-looking site and tweaked it along the way.

But if you don't get started now, you may still have nothing this time next year.

What do you need on your author website?

Once you get your site up and running, start by setting up these basics.

Home page with introductory text about you and your books

If people have come to your site via a link to a blog post, the Home or About page will likely be the next page they look at. Visuals are critically important, so include your book covers and images that resonate with your target audience.

About page

This includes your official bio as well as a more personal introduction. Include a short version that can be used for interviews and speaker introductions as well as your professional author photo. You can also include pictures that give a glimpse into your life, as well as your social media links.

An email list sign-up

More on this in the next chapter.

Book pages with buy buttons for all formats and all sites

I have individual book pages as well as a main one from the menu bar, so the reader can always find details of my books and links to the appropriate stores, as well as how to buy direct.

You're welcome to model my books page at:
www.TheCreativePenn.com/books

Contact page

You need to have some way that people can connect with you. Set up an email account specifically for your author name.

I use GSuite which provides email for websites, and I have different author emails per brand. You can also use a form on your Contact page, which will lessen the amount of junk mail you get. I use Gravity Forms.

* * *

Those are the main things you need, but you might also like to include:

Events and appearances

If you're a professional speaker or run events, list those on a specific page and include links for people to book them. You could also have a Speaker page with booking details, testimonials, video, and a list of your topics.

Regular content

You can incorporate your blog, videos, or podcast as part of your website, which I recommend if you want to drive traffic over time. More on this in chapter 5.8 on content marketing.

Press page or media kit

The phrase 'media kit' sounds pretty scary, like it's some complicated tool that only certain people understand. But actually, it's just information to help journalists and bloggers.

Add your contact details and your agent if you have one. Include phone numbers if you want to, as journalists often want instant access, although you may prefer to keep this private. You'll also need a short bio and long bio; professional pictures with headshots and action shots that can be used with photo credit details if necessary; a list of awards, endorsements, press coverage or media quotes if you have them; links to your books and cover images; sample interview questions; and a one-pager on each book.

Over time, you will be featured in various media, so collect those clips and use 'As featured in' on your home page as social proof. We are tribal creatures, and this social proof might make a difference to whether people are interested in buying your books or giving you their attention.

If you're just starting out, you may feel this will never happen. But trust me, if you keep creating consistently over time, you will get this kind of opportunity, so it pays to be prepared.

Next steps

Once you have a home base on the Internet, you can direct everything else back to it. Update all your social media profiles, add your site to physical marketing materials like business cards and postcards, add your site to the back matter of your ebooks and include it on the back cover of print books, and add it to your email signature.

Remember to keep your website updated with new books over time, because it's how readers, journalists, agents and publishers can always find you.

Questions:

- Do you have a website already? Is the domain name appropriate for a long-term career?

- What do you need on your author website? What could you improve if you already have one?

Resources:

- Tutorial on how to build your own author website in under 30 minutes: www.TheCreativePenn.com/authorwebsite

- Tutorial on how to set up the Author Pro WordPress Theme: www.TheCreativePenn.com/ setup-author-pro-theme

5.6 Build an email list

Everyone talks about building an email list, but why is it so important, especially for non-fiction writers who want to build a business around a book?

Control over income and a direct relationship with customers

If you have an email list of people who have given you permission to contact them, you have a way to reach readers and fans when you have a new book or product out, and that gives you **more control over sales and income**.

You are not entirely dependent on Amazon selling your book, or Facebook serving your ad, or algorithms changing, or Google putting you on page one of search. You can always reach your customers directly.

You can also **build up a relationship with readers** over time, so they get to know you. Email is a great way to communicate and is much more direct, targeted and relational than social media. I consider email to be a huge part of my direct marketing efforts and spend time every day answering email from readers and my community.

Owning your email list is about true independence, the ability to sell your books even if all the book sales websites disappeared. If you're traditionally published, it's the ability to walk away from a publisher without fear, because you know you have an audience you can reach yourself.

If you're on your first book, you may see building an email

list as an insurmountable challenge. But if you start a list with book one, then you will have at least a handful of people to tell about book two. We all start at zero, and your list will grow over time as readers find you, or if you actively promote it.

The best time to start building an email list is right now, wherever you are on the author journey.

What will you offer in exchange for an email address?

Many authors have a sign-up for a newsletter on their website, but as a reader, do you really want another newsletter cluttering up your inbox? Think about what is useful, entertaining or inspirational for your target market. What would they value?

For non-fiction authors, you could give away a PDF of useful tips, excerpted chapters or one of your books, free video training or audios. If you sign up for my Author 2.0 Blueprint, you receive a free ebook as well as a number of video and email tutorials.

You don't have to start with the most amazing thing ever. You can build up your offer over time. I started out with a one-page PDF of tips, but over the years, I've improved the Blueprint and the accompanying email sequence. Get started where you are, and you can change it up over time.

If you want to give away a book, I use and highly recommend BookFunnel.com for delivering free books as part of the email list sign-up process. You can also use it for sending Advance Reader Copies to your early readers, and they can watermark the ebooks if you're concerned about piracy. They allow books to be delivered to any digital device and handle customer service for technically challenged readers.

How to set up your list

The first step is to **sign up for a list management service,** because you can't just email people from your personal account. I recommend ConvertKit because it's easy to use if you're starting out, but also has scalable functionality for those who have a more developed business. I use it for all three of my author names and websites.

Watch my tutorial and get a cheatsheet on how to set up your email list with ConvertKit at www.TheCreativePenn. com/setup-email-list

Other recommended services include MailChimp, Aweber, or MailerLite, and there are more emerging all the time. Compare the various services to see what would suit you best.

Create a sign-up form using one of the templates from the email service. Once you've customized it, they will give you a little piece of code to copy and paste into your website. It will appear as a sign-up form that readers can use to enter their email and start the process of receiving messages from you. You can put it at the top of the page, on the sidebar, on a special page, in a pop-up, or all of these at once. It's up to you.

You also need to **set up a sequence of emails for subscribers**, also known as autoresponders, which go out automatically when someone signs up.

This might be as simple as one they receive straight away with your free offer, or you might have a whole sequence that guides them through a process. My Author 2.0 Blueprint sequence has a series of weekly emails describing how to write, publish and market books as well as make a living from your writing. These are useful for the reader but also enable them to get to know, like and trust me so they might be interested in buying a book or course at some point.

Each email list service also provides a **Broadcast mechanism** to send newsletters or notification of sales, events or book launches. They have templates you can use so you can drag and drop images in – no need for a complicated set-up anymore!

Test your sign-up form and emails with a test account and send yourself a Broadcast just to make sure that everything is OK. Then you're ready to go!

Add the sign-up to the back of your books

You're in the best position to ask a reader to join your list when they have just finished your book (and hopefully loved it!). If you're traditionally published, it's worth asking your publisher if you can include a link to your email list at the back of the book. Pitch it as being useful for connecting with readers and making marketing easier for the next book.

You can use a clickable link in ebooks and an easy-to-type URL in print books. It's also a good idea to have a URL that's easy to say out loud, as you can then mention it on podcasts, in interviews and when speaking. Take any chance you can to tell people about it.

Remember, sign-ups will be a trickle at first, but your list will grow over time, just like everything else in the author business.

What do you include in your Broadcast emails?

Once you start building a list of email subscribers, you need to keep talking to them. Some authors get stressed over what they're meant to send, but this will differ depending on what you promised at sign-up and also what you are doing with your author business as a whole.

Non-fiction authors tend to use email marketing more regularly, because it is a major source of income through affiliate commission, consulting or product sales, rather than books alone.

You could include **news and articles** about your industry or niche; **articles, audio or video** which might include personal items like photos from your research trips; details about your **new book** or product releases; **book reviews** related to your niche; or **competitions,** giveaways and anything else relevant to your audience.

You want people to open your email, so make it interesting and **include a headline** that will make them want to read on. **You need to send emails regularly** enough that it is not a surprise when you do send one.

Don't just email when you have something to sell. Build a relationship over time. Fans want to know what you're up to, and they will be interested in what you have to share with them.

But there are no rules!

The bare minimum is to simply have a list of people to notify when your next book comes out, and then you can improve your communication over time. Remember, every name on that list is a person, so think about connecting with them on a personal level.

Build a Street Team

Some of the people on your email list will be super-fans who read all your books and love everything you do. They will be a small sub-set but they are the ones you want to engage with more regularly, so it's worth setting up what's known as a Street Team.

This is a group within your main email list who get your Advance Review Copies (ARCs) before official release and help you by reviewing the book or spreading the word on blogs and social media. You can build this smaller sub-set by emailing the main list and asking them to apply.

Use your email list in paid advertising

Your email list can be incredibly useful for paid advertising. You can load a list of emails into Facebook, and they will create an Audience for you to advertise to, while still adhering to data protection laws. When I email my list about a new book, I also do an ad to the list audience at the same time. Readers often need exposure multiple times before they buy.

You can also create a LookaLike audience, where Facebook find other similar people who you can advertise to, attracting more people to your list over time. Your ads will likely be cheaper if you use your list and a LookaLike, so it's well worth incorporating this step into your marketing strategy.

Use email marketing with integrity

Seth Godin, author of many marketing books, describes permission marketing as "the privilege (not the right) of delivering anticipated, personal and relevant messages to people who actually want to get them."

In 2018, data integrity became even more important with the revelations around Cambridge Analytica and Facebook data, as well as the EU General Data Protection Regulation (GDPR) regulations. Trust is critical in your relationship with email subscribers, and you also need to be legally compliant and ethical in your email marketing. Here are some tips:

Don't add people to your list manually.

People should actively opt-in by signing up themselves in exchange for something specific. Activate double-opt-in on your list, which means people sign up and then click a Confirm link by email before they get emails. This is an anti-spam mechanism that helps to ensure permission.

Don't buy lists

Those people have not specifically asked for information from you. I get spam emails every day from people who have signed me up to lists with an email I never use for that type of thing. I delete and block them immediately.

Include a privacy policy on your website

It should explain how you will interact, what you will send, and whether you use cookies on your site. There are lots of templates online that you can modify for your website.

Respect your list

Keep their details private. Don't sell or share your list with anyone else. Be a valuable resource to your subscribers by providing the information, inspiration or entertainment that they signed up. You never want to be seen as a spammer, so give away great information, offer quality on a regular basis for free, and people will be happy to buy from you when you have something they are interested in.

Adhere to anti-spam and data protection guidelines

Use a physical mailing address in the footer of the email (you can use a PO Box or other address). Ensure there is a clear unsubscribe button, and that you have a way to delete their data.

But don't let these guidelines freak you out and stop you from developing your email list. They are positive rules that enhance data protection and are not hard to abide by. Use one of the approved email list providers as they all have ways to help you adhere to these guidelines.

Questions:

- Why is having your own email list so important?

- What can you offer your readers that they will value in exchange for signing up?

- Have you researched the different email services and decided what would work best for you?

- Have you set up a sign-up form and put it on your website and in the back of your book? Have you tested your sign-up?

- Have you set up an automated email sequence for when people sign up?

- Have you decided what will go in your Broadcast emails?

- Do you understand how to use email marketing with integrity?

Resources:

- Tutorial on setting up your email list signup:
  www.TheCreativePenn.com/setup-email-list

- ConvertKit email service:
  www.TheCreativePenn.com/convert

- Sign up for the Author 2.0 Blueprint:
  www.TheCreativePenn.com/blueprint

- ConvertKit GDPR guidelines:
  www.TheCreativePenn.com/GDPR

5.7 Integrate email marketing with your book

Most non-fiction authors will have other products or services around their book or at least be planning some in the future. But when a book is sold on one of the retail stores, you don't know who that customer is. So how do you get them on your email list so that you can develop a relationship and hopefully sell more of your products/services over time?

(1) Include a Call to Action in your book for the reader to sign up for an extra ebook or updates

This is the most basic email integration you can do – and you should be doing at least this much. All my non-fiction books include a link to sign up for my free Author 2.0 Blueprint at:

www.TheCreativePenn.com/blueprint

It leads people into a sequence of automated emails that link to useful resources, affiliate links and products.

(2) Include links in your book for extra bonuses

In an interview on The Creative Penn Podcast, Joseph Alexander explained his email marketing design for his guitar books, which he sells primarily in print.

"After the introduction, there's a How To Get The Audio section. I give away the audio recordings of each [guitar] example in the book. If you want to get the audio, you go to my website, stick your email address in, choose your book, and then you get access to your audio. That means we know which book they bought."

Joseph has an automated email sequence per book offering extra lessons and then funnels each customer into what they might like to buy next. It's a self-sustaining method of sales, but it does require a lot of books and products, as well as a very organized system of emails. Something to aspire to, perhaps!

Of course, if you don't have music books, you can do this with an indirect call to action within the book as I have done with resources throughout this book. A certain percentage of readers will go to the website or the podcast or the YouTube channel and will find the material useful and will enter my ecosystem that way.

(3) Sell direct

You can sell directly from your website using services like Selz, PayHip, Spotify, or PayPal, which will collect the customer email and physical address, and provide you with more revenue per transaction.

You can use BookFunnel.com to deliver the ebook to the reader's device and use an automation service like Zapier. com to integrate with your email provider. You can then develop a series of email sequences to lead people into other books and courses.

The main issue with this is that most readers want to buy from established retail stores and you need a lot of traffic to your site to generate even a small percentage of direct sales. But this type of direct sale is becoming more common as authors focus on building their personal brand and business ecosystem.

Questions:

- How can you integrate email marketing into your book?

- What are some of the tools you might need to investigate further?

Resources:

- Interview with Joseph Alexander on his print-focused publishing model and email funnel: www.TheCreativePenn.com/joseph

- Direct sales platforms: Selz.com, PayHip.com, PayPal direct, Shopify.com

- Delivery of ebook to customer's device: www.BookFunnel.com

- Automation service: zapier.com

5.8 Content marketing for non-fiction books

"You can buy attention (advertising). You can beg for attention from the media (PR). You can bug people one at a time to get attention (sales). Or you can earn attention by creating something interesting and valuable and then publishing it online for free."

David Meerman Scott, The New Rules of Marketing and PR

Let's be clear. You do not have to use blogging, podcasting, video or social media in order to sell books.

But if you want to build a platform that you own over time, where traffic eventually comes to you for free, where you are truly independent, then it's worth considering.

Content marketing is creating and sharing online material like articles, audio, video and images that don't explicitly market products but instead attract attention to your website or profile. Some of the people who check out that content may sign up to join your email list or follow you, and may eventually buy your books or products.

It's an attraction form of marketing.

Each piece of content you put out there is another way for people to find you, another breadcrumb that might lead someone to your book. By spreading your content across different media, you will be able to target a variety of audiences.

Can you give away too much for free?

Some people worry about putting too much out there for free, but the more you give away, the more people can find you, and customers often prefer everything to be packaged up in book format, or in courses or other products. Or they want to hire you to do it for them. I've certainly found this to be true in my business.

I have several thousand articles, videos, and audio recordings on my site, all bringing people in from different corners of the Internet. You can get 99% of what I do for free on my various channels, but I still make a multi-six-figure income from my writing thanks to people like you who buy. [Thank you!]

Content marketing vs. social media

With content marketing, you create something original. You own it, and you host it somewhere that you control. This content lasts a long time and continues to be relevant. It can be found in search engines, and people may consume it or link back to it even years later. For example, people who discover my podcast on iTunes often go back and listen to years of backlist interviews, because the content is mostly evergreen.

Social media is ephemeral, designed to catch attention at the point when someone is present in the moment. Posts on Facebook, Twitter, Instagram and other social media only appear briefly on timelines and then sink into the noise. Anything on social media is immediate and fades fast.

You also don't own the platform, and you should never build your entire platform on someone else's online real estate because when the rules change, your business will be impacted.

You can use social media to amplify the reach of your content marketing, but the two are fundamentally different things.

Types of content marketing

When considering what types of content to create, it's a good idea to start with what you already use. Have do you currently consume information, entertainment or inspiration? What would it make sense for you to produce?

Text-based articles and blog posts

Blogging changed my life, and I still recommend it for **finding your author voice**, **attracting your target market**, and learning how to press Publish regularly to get your words out into the world.

It also helps you **build a reputation**. When I'm researching people, I will always go to their blog to see what they're writing about.

You can write on your own site, guest post on more established sites, and/or write articles and post them on Facebook, Medium, LinkedIn and other high-traffic sites. Text-based content marketing has certainly not disappeared, but it has become harder to get attention with it.

Ensure you have **clear, customer-focused headlines** that make people want to read on, well-formatted articles with sub-headings, **white space, good use of images** as well as shareable links. I use Social Warfare, a premium social media plug-in that enables me to use images and add social media buttons to the posts.

If you don't want to blog on your own site, **guest posting** can be effective for non-fiction authors, in particular – but only if you target specific niche sites with high traffic. Many of these sites have long waiting lists, so pitch them early with several ideas for headlines that their target market will enjoy. Always focus on delivering value.

Check out my blog: www.TheCreativePenn.com/blog

Podcasting and audio

"There's a level of dedication that comes from podcast listeners that you otherwise don't find, and now the numbers prove it. Podcasts aren't a bubble, they're a boom – and that boom is only getting louder."

Miranda Katz, Wired magazine

A podcast is audio content distributed over the Internet. Podcasts can be talk shows, interviews, teaching, rants or indeed, anything else you fancy producing in audio format.

The main advantage of podcasts is that listeners can download the audio whenever they want, instead of radio, which is available at a specific time of day. People can discover audio at any time, and if they connect with the host, they are likely to download backlist episodes, which makes it evergreen content.

As a listener, you can subscribe to a show, and then episodes will download automatically to your device. The most common podcast players are iTunes, Stitcher and various apps on the Android platform, but there are lots of different ways to listen. I love podcasts and listen to a number every week while walking, doing chores or cooking. I skim blog posts and social media for information, but I deep dive on podcasts!

The consumption of audiobooks and podcasts has grown with the expansion of smartphones and faster Internet download speeds. This will only continue to grow, as the Internet is expected to reach everyone in the world by 2025, and there are smart phones that cost less than $5 in India. The English-language audio market is expanding, and in fact, my podcast has listeners in over 200 countries and over 2.5 million downloads at the time of writing. Pretty crazy!

Podcasting is a significant investment of time, but it's also a powerful way to build a loyal fanbase. Anyone who listens to your voice every week will become a fan if you share your personal story, smile and bring people into your world. You can also connect with influencers in your niche, as they are far more likely to talk to you if you have an audience that will help them reach new potential customers.

When you interview someone, they will often link to that interview from their site as well as sharing it through their social networks. If your interviewees have a large network and a well-ranking site, this can increase your site's authority, and over the long term, all those incoming links improve your ranking and therefore, your ability to be discovered online.

If you have your own podcast, make sure to include show notes and/or a transcript to help with Search Engine Optimization. At the time of writing, audio cannot be indexed, so you need other ways of optimizing for search traffic. I use Speechpad.com for transcription.

If you don't want to go as far as producing your own podcast, you can pitch other podcasters to have you on as a guest. Make sure you're a good fit for the show by listening to a number of episodes in advance and then crafting a personal email that makes it clear what value you can offer their audience.

Check out The Creative Penn Podcast on iTunes and other apps, or find the backlist and subscription links at:

www.TheCreativePenn.com/podcast

Video marketing

"You're looking into the eyes of your viewers
when you talk to a camera. You understand them.
You help them. You relate to them. That is all vlogging is.
It's being human on camera."

Amy Schmittauer, Vlog Like a Boss

YouTube is owned by Google and is either the #1 or #2 search engine on any given day. YouTube has over a billion users, and over 500 million hours of video are watched on it every day. *Forbes* reported in 2017 that a third of all time spent online is dedicated to video. *Inc* magazine reported that by 2019, video will account for 80% of all Internet traffic.

If you have a lot of videos on a particular topic, your channel will become a place that people subscribe and return to. People are also increasingly used to consuming long-form video on YouTube as more TV shows are available for streaming.

Video is great for **instant connection**. If people know you, like you and trust you, they are more likely to buy your book. When people see your face and your smile, when they hear your voice, they will make a decision as to whether they like you. The greatest proportion of human communication is non-verbal, which can't be communicated in plain text, but is clear in video.

Video can **drive traffic** to your main author site if you add show notes under the video or a website link in the video. This increases your traffic and hopefully your email subscriber list and sales.

It helps you **stand out** because so few authors produce video. It is especially valuable if you want to speak or if you have a business that goes beyond the book.

If you're someone who enjoys video and can **commit to regular production**, it can be a fantastic form of content marketing. You can talk directly to the camera in the vlogging style of the top YouTubers, or you could also do interviews, presentations, tutorials with screen-sharing, on-location videos as I do for book research trips, mini-films with music and voice-over and anything else you can think of. Go down the rabbit hole of YouTube and you'll soon get lots of ideas.

You can also **integrate video with social media** by doing Facebook live video and then upload the video to YouTube later, or vice versa. I record my videos and then upload them directly to Facebook as well as YouTube. You can use video engagement as a way to target advertising, so it's a great way to **repurpose your content**.

I produce videos every week on writing craft and business, as well as sharing interviews with other creatives.

Check out my channel:

www.YouTube.com/thecreativepenn

Image marketing

All your content should have a shareable image attached, but some content marketers focus entirely on the image platforms like Pinterest or Instagram for the foundation of their business. Infographics may suit some authors, or use photos, shareable quote images or anything else you can think of.

Use canva.com to get appropriate sizing for all your graphics.

Integrate your best content with email marketing and social media

Once you have created valuable content for your audience, you need to make sure it can be found. Use landing pages on your site so you can list the best content, for example, www.TheCreativePenn.com/publishing is my landing page for my best content on publishing.

Use those pages inside your email sequences to direct people once they sign up for your mailing list. Regularly share links to your landing pages in social media with clickable headlines and eye-catching images. You can also use those links inside your books, as I have done throughout this one.

This kind of set-up takes time to build, but it can be hugely effective for driving a continuous cycle of traffic, sales and revenue over time.

Monetizing content marketing

This is where the business model of the non-fiction author really comes into its own because once you have an ecosystem of content alongside email marketing, books, products, and services, you can start to make multiple streams of income from your content.

You can serve your community by being useful, entertaining or inspirational, but you can also make an income that grows based on your traffic over time.

Add **affiliate links** to your content, starting with something as basic as Amazon's affiliate program for book links, and moving into useful services and products.

Add a **Patreon subscription** to your podcast or YouTube channel, so that fans can support you.

Look for **advertising revenue** from companies that fit your brand or enable ads on YouTube.

And of course, you can integrate **your own books, products and services** into your content along the way.

For an example of this, check out my landing page and video tutorial for how to find and work with a professional editor:

www.TheCreativePenn.com/how-to-find-and-work-with-professional-editors

This provides useful information for my audience but also gives me an opportunity to talk about my books, and I link to a page with affiliate links on.

Tips for effective content marketing

Understand what your target market wants. Then dominate that niche by producing specific, high-quality content that will be relevant for the long term.

Learn copywriting skills around headlines and how content is structured online. Writing a book is very different to writing a blog post that results in the reader taking action, and you need to understand both.

Be consistent. My podcast used to be ad hoc, but when I switched to a weekly show, the engagement and traffic took off. If you produce consistently over time, you will build your book sales and your online platform. All I have done is write pretty much every day, podcast, blog and share regularly, and over the years, it has built up to something significant.

The power of compounding in action!

Be authentic. Share your journey and your ups and downs. People will resonate with that so much more than a stilted business-like persona. Make sure you always share your own spin on particular topics, don't just share other people's ideas. In the end, readers will connect with your personality and your voice.

Remember social karma. Be generous. Share other people's material more than your own. Give before you expect to receive. Use social media to connect with influencers and be useful to them before asking for anything in return.

Is it worth the time to build a platform based on content marketing?

For me, it's absolutely been worth it, as my multi-six-figure business is built on the back of content at The Creative Penn. It's the engine that drives my revenue streams, and it's far more secure than relying on the vagaries of algorithms or my writing speed to power my income.

I have a lot of information available for free, but I also have books, courses and services I recommend for those who want to take it further. I travel the world as a professional speaker as a result of building my platform online, and I love the work I do. I blog, podcast, make videos and share on social media because I still continue to find value in it. I'm even taking the lessons I've learned into my fiction world because it's been so effective.

But you have to consider what you want for the long term and what effort you want to put in. Do you want to build a long-term business? Or do you just have one book you want to get into the world and then move on?

Questions:

- Why is content marketing a good option for non-fiction authors?

- What's the difference between content marketing and social media? How can the two work together?

- What are the different types of content marketing?

- What would suit you best and why?

- How could you consider monetizing your content?

- How can you make the most of whichever option you decide? What are your next steps?

Resources:

- *The New Rules of Marketing and PR: How to Use Social Media, Online Video, Mobile Applications, Blogs, News Releases, and Viral Marketing to Reach Buyers Directly* – David Meerman Scott

- The Creative Penn Blog:
  www.TheCreativePenn.com/blog

- The Creative Penn YouTube channel:
  www.YouTube.com/thecreativepenn

- Social Warfare plug-in for WordPress: www.warfareplugins.com

- Wired article on podcasting, Jan 2018: www.wired.com/story/apple-podcast-analytics-first-month

- Transcription service: www.speechpad.com

- The Creative Penn Podcast subscription and backlist episodes: www.TheCreativePenn.com/podcast

- *Vlog Like a Boss: How to Kill It Online with Video Blogging* – Amy Schmittauer

- Inc article on video marketing: https://www.inc.com/gordon-tredgold/20-reasons-why-you-should-boost-your-video-marketing-budget-in-2017.html

- Forbes article on video marketing: https://www.forbes.com/sites/forbesagencycouncil/2017/02/03/video-marketing-the-future-of-content-marketing/#139365016b53

- Image creation for social sharing: www.canva.com

5.9 My non-fiction marketing journey

If any of this is overwhelming, then remember that you can learn marketing just as much as any other skill. You can also find types of marketing that suit your personality, so whether you're into data analysis and algorithms, networking in person, helping people or just writing a lot, there are options for you.

This chapter goes through my marketing journey, what has worked for me, and my lessons learned along the way. Of course, this is anecdotal, and you will have to find the things that suit you and your book, but hopefully this helps give you an idea of how an integrated marketing approach works as part of a long-term author career.

Starting out with the first book

I self-published my first book, *How to Enjoy Your Job or Find a New One*, in early 2008. I was living in Brisbane, Australia and this was before the international Kindle, so ebooks had not gone mainstream. The iPhone was new, YouTube was mainly LOLcatz, Myspace was the place to be and Twitter was just emerging. Bloggers had just started to make money and Web 2.0 was the catchphrase of the emerging social web.

Self-publishing then meant printing books and selling them yourself. I was so excited about my book that I ordered 2000 and had them delivered to our house, certain that I would sell them all, make loads of money and become a bestseller ...

Unfortunately, like many authors starting out, I didn't know anything about marketing. Those books sat in our house in boxes, evidence of my failure to understand that being an author is not just about writing – it's also about getting those books into the hands of readers.

But I love learning and I love a challenge, so I started researching book marketing. I read books and took courses – which in those days were sent as a packet of CDs and hard-copy workbooks – and I also attended live events.

Traditional media was still the main marketing route, alongside direct physical mail, so I decided to learn about press releases with the aim of getting on TV and radio. After a lot of focus, I made it into local and national papers, along with appearances on Australian national radio and national TV.

It was an ego boost but I only sold a couple of books, so it wasn't worth the effort. I started to speak professionally, learning from the National Speakers' Association, but then I realised that I could only reach people in my area in person. It wasn't enough, especially as I was working a day job that left me exhausted.

There had to be a better way.

Tip: **Find a marketing method that fits with your lifestyle and personality.**

Discovering Internet marketing

In 2008, blogging was starting to emerge as more than just personal journals online. It was becoming the heart of online businesses, driving traffic to sell products and services over the Internet. I discovered a blogging community who taught others, like Yaro Starak of Entrepreneur's Journey, Darren Rowse of Problogger, and Brian, Sonia and the team at Copyblogger. I decided to focus on Internet marketing.

In December 2008, I set up TheCreativePenn.com, my third blog and the one that finally stuck. The other two were related to that first book and I swiftly grew bored of them.

Tip: **Don't build a site you will grow out of.** Choose a domain name that will last. Your name is a good start.

If you go to the Wayback Machine at archive.org/web, you can see the original version of my site. It was super-ugly, but it got the job done and we all have to start somewhere! I built the site using WordPress and over time, I have changed Themes (the look and feel of the site), but the core is still the same.

Tip: **Learn how to use WordPress.** A small investment in time will keep your costs down. Check out my tutorial on building your own website at:

www.TheCreativePenn.com/authorwebsite

Setting up my core marketing systems

I listened to a lot of downloadable audio at the time – it wasn't even called podcasting back then. You downloaded an mp3 file to your computer, transferred it to a player and then listened.

I commuted for an hour or so every day, first by car and later on the train, so I learned by listening. I distinctly remember driving along the motorway one day. The sun was shining (as it did a lot in Brisbane), but I was miserable in my job and I resented going into the office. I needed to change my life.

That day, I listened to an audio recording of Yaro Starak talking about how he was able to work from home, look after his family, travel and make more than enough money. He had just bought a house with his income from blogging. I wanted that freedom, so I decided to model myself on Yaro. I did his (fantastic) course and started to put it into action.

[You can still learn from Yaro. Check out his up-to-date Blog Profits Blueprint at:
www.TheCreativePenn.com/blogblueprint]

Tip: **Find people to model** who are ahead of you on the entrepreneurial journey that you seek to follow.

I started blogging on what I learned about writing, self-publishing and Internet marketing and after a few months, I started to attract readers, other authors like me who were just starting out. I was able to reach more people with my own site online than I could reach with national media. I set up an email list, with the first iteration of my Author 2.0 Blueprint as a lead magnet.

I started doing audio, with my first interview going out on 15 March 2009. I started doing video on YouTube, and also joined Twitter in January 2009. If you go back and look at those early episodes, it's pretty embarrassing, but you have to start somewhere and learn along the way.

Tip: **If you don't have a budget for the perfect set-up, get started anyway!**

You can do video with your smartphone or directly into your computer and you can do audio easily now with free Skype. Don't wait until everything is perfect. Get started and learn along the way.

Developing an integrated, repeatable marketing approach

"The secret of your success is in your daily routine."

Darren Hardy, The Compound Effect

I'm still using the same marketing channels ten years later. I have a website with an email list – I update the Author 2.0 Blueprint every few months. I blog several times a week, I have a podcast, a YouTube channel and I use Twitter as my main social media platform.

So while some things have changed and developed, my core marketing approach has remained the same. This is critical in understanding how marketing works for the long term, because it all compounds over time.

A little every day or every week adds to the ways that people can discover you. It brings readers into your ecosystem and then they might discover your books, products or services along the way. It might feel like you are getting nowhere at first, but if you persist, things start to speed up. Your traffic grows, your income grows, your reputation grows and opportunities expand.

But only if you are consistent over time.

The most common issue I see amongst those seeking this kind of career is giving up too soon.

Tip: **Find what you enjoy and integrate marketing into your life.** Understand that it compounds over time.

The Kindle goes international and ebooks go mainstream

So I was building an online platform that started to make me some money from online sales of my existing book and a course I made, plus I was attracting speaking events. I loved writing, but I couldn't understand how I could possibly make a living from books, as they were so hard to sell and distribute.

Then in October 2009, I bought one of the first Kindles to arrive in Australia, part of the first wave of international devices. Although it had been available in the US from late 2007, it wasn't until it went international that I became aware of how it could change the possibilities for authors. Non-US authors couldn't publish direct on KDP at that time, and in my review video, I talk about publishing through a friend in the US to get my books up there. You can tell I'm a little in love with it in the video!

Watch the video:

www.TheCreativePenn.com/international_kindle

Those of you who follow my podcast know that I'm a bit of a futurist, always excited about how new technologies can help creatives. I saw the future in the Kindle device because I could sell books to people all over the world by just uploading a file. That same year, Booksurge became Createspace, Amazon's print-on-demand service, so it was possible to sell print books globally without the overheads of printing, warehousing and shipping.

This made Internet marketing just as useful for selling books as online products and services. And that's when I realized that it was truly possible to make a living as an author in this new world.

This was the beginning of Kindle marketing, the early days of indies like Amanda Hocking and John Locke, when J.A. Konrath started blogging about the new world, when putting a book at 99c could help you hit the bestseller lists and sell millions of copies. It was the Wild West, covers were generally terrible and readers devoured everything because there weren't very many ebooks. It was the beginning of the book-centered marketing approach that many use today.

I continued writing, blogging, podcasting and using social media, as well as writing more books, creating more products and speaking professionally – all while working my consulting day job.

In 2011, I left my job to become a full-time author entrepreneur, and in 2015, the business hit six figures. You can find more detail on my business model in *How to Make a Living with your Writing.*

My current marketing ecosystem

People always want to know what's new and working right now, but the core of my marketing these days is exactly the same as it was at the very beginning. It's designed to be an ecosystem that continues to grow and expand as I add more books and more content over time.

Book-centered marketing:

I write multiple books in a series for a niche audience (authors), using branded covers with a consistent look under a specific non-fiction author name, Joanna Penn. The book titles or sub-titles are search engine optimized so readers can find them by searching. They clearly tell the reader what they will get. My books are available in ebook, print and audiobook formats and have sold in 89 countries in English.

I choose categories and keywords that best represent the books and use tools like KDP Rocket to find more keywords to use in paid advertising. I run Amazon Ads, I use Kobo Writing Life promotions, and I use periodic Facebook ads, BookBub and other paid advertising options as they emerge.

Successful Self-Publishing is a free ebook on all platforms which attracts people to the other books in my series and has links to my website for extra help, as well as a sign-up to my email list through the Author 2.0 Blueprint: www. TheCreativePenn.com/blueprint

Author-centered marketing:

I focus almost exclusively on Internet marketing because it's global and scalable, meaning I can reach people all over the world from my laptop. It suits my lifestyle and introvert personality and I like to focus on being useful. If I can attract a target market with free helpful information given in a generous manner, some of those people will buy from me.

The core of my non-fiction business is my website, TheCreativePenn.com, built on WordPress and a premium theme, which mean it's easily upgradable and my costs stay low over time. I use a hosting service and back the site up externally so it can't be turned off and I can restore it if it's hacked.

I have specific pages for my email sign-up, books, audiobooks and courses, and then landing pages for other affiliate products and services which all drive revenue. I use content marketing to drive traffic to the site – articles every week on the blog, weekly podcast interviews and YouTube videos. I use social media to spread the word about the content. I use email marketing to stay in touch with readers and automated email sequences to drive people through useful content and showcase my books and products.

My content continues to build my brand.

For example, those who listen to the podcast every week will often share the episode on social media or talk about it to others. My short videos on craft and business on YouTube are useful, easily shareable and build my brand.

I also do a lot of interviews on other podcasts, my primary

mechanism for reaching a wider audience. I still do occasional professional speaking and attend live events, although I'm reducing these to focus more on writing, podcasts, and video as I can reach more people that way.

This type of integrated marketing system does take some organizing to set up, but if you can develop a process flow, utilize scheduling and automation tools, and work with a virtual assistant and/or other freelancers, then you will find yourself free to write the books of your heart – or just go lie in the hammock and read.

You have to start somewhere, as I did, and improve things over time. Back in 2008, I could never have imagined that I would be running a creative business like this ten years later. It's all about creating consistently and taking action every day toward your goal.

"Consistency is the key to achieving and maintaining momentum."

Darren Hardy, The Compound Effect

Launching a book into this ecosystem

A podcast host asked me the other day how I stay energized during the launch of a book as he'd heard so many authors complaining about the amount of work they have to do on launch.

But a launch is not really a big deal for me anymore because my business model does not rely on spike sales in the first week or month of publication. It's about sustained sales over years to come, as people trickle through the various funnels I have. After all, a book is new to the person who has just discovered it, whenever that happens to be, and I keep earning all the time.

The spike launch approach is common in traditional publishing, where in-store sales and promotional activity happens all at once before resources are tasked with marketing the next book in the queue, but it's just not necessary as an independent author.

My launches these days consist of a few key things. I talk about the process of writing and researching and publishing on my podcast and social media, often sharing pictures when appropriate. This creates an expectation and an awareness of the upcoming book. I set up a pre-order so I can capture early sales, particularly useful for iBooks and Kobo and also good for getting everything organized before the go-live date. I send the book out to a few key readers in advance for early reviews.

On launch day, I email my list with the links, as well as announcing it on the podcast, YouTube channel and on social media. I schedule paid ads and social media shares across the various channels for the first week or so. I may also go on other podcasts. But then I'll return to the baseline level of what I do every week regardless of whether there is a launch or not. It's that momentum that drives my business.

* * *

I hope my journey demonstrates that you can start with nothing and build an ecosystem over time, learning as you go, integrating different aspects of marketing with your growing author business and multiple streams of income.

And that's the important thing.

Because there is no point in marketing unless you have something to sell.

So get back to finishing your book!

For more detail on book marketing, check out *How to Market a Book*, available in ebook, print and audiobook formats.

Questions:

- How can you shift your mindset to a longer-term view? What do you want to achieve in the next 10 years and how can you start now?

- What lessons or tips are useful for your journey?

Resources:

- *How to Market a Book* – Joanna Penn

- *How to Make a Living with your Writing* – Joanna Penn

- My favorite sites for professional bloggers: Entrepreneurs-Journey.com, Problogger.com, Copyblogger.com

- Yaro Starak's up-to-date Blog Profits Blueprint at: www.TheCreativePenn.com/blogblueprint

- Wayback Machine at http://archive.org/web/

- My tutorial on how to build your own website at: www.TheCreativePenn.com/authorwebsite

- *The Compound Effect: Jumpstart Your Income, Your Life, Your Success* – Darren Hardy

- My video on the international Kindle from 2009: www.TheCreativePenn.com/international_kindle

Conclusion

"Your body of work is everything you create, contribute, affect, and impact. For individuals, it is the personal legacy you leave at the end of your life, including all the tangible and intangible things you have created. Individuals who structure their careers around autonomy, mastery, and purpose will have a powerful body of work."

Pamela Slim, Body of Work:
Finding the Thread that Ties Your Story Together

As I wrote this book, I revisited my journals from 12 years ago. I was miserable in my job, desperately trying to work out what I wanted to do with my life. The person I was back then does not exist anymore and my transformation into a happy creative making a living with my writing all stemmed from the decision I made to write my first non-fiction book.

So, if you're still hesitating about writing and publishing your book, please take that first step. It will change your life and then you can go on and change other people's.

Happy writing!

Need more help on your author journey?

Sign up for my *free* Author 2.0 Blueprint and email series, and receive monthly updates on writing, publishing, book marketing, and making a living with your writing:

www.TheCreativePenn.com/blueprint

* * *

Check out my multi-media course, *How to Write Non-Fiction*, and join my private Facebook group where you can ask questions and meet other writers:

www.TheCreativePenn.com/writenonfiction

About Joanna Penn

Joanna Penn is an Award-nominated, New York Times and USA Today bestselling author of thrillers under J.F.Penn and also writes non-fiction for authors. She's an award-winning entrepreneur, podcaster, and YouTuber.

Her site, TheCreativePenn.com has been voted in the Top 100 sites for writers by Writer's Digest. Joanna also has a popular podcast for writers, The Creative Penn.

Joanna has a Master's degree in Theology from the University of Oxford, Mansfield College, and a Graduate Diploma in Psychology from the University of Auckland, New Zealand.

She lives in Bath, England but spent 11 years living in Australia and New Zealand. Joanna enjoys traveling as often as possible. She's interested in religion and psychology and loves to read, drink gin and tonic, and soak up European culture through art, architecture and food.

Connect with Joanna:

www.TheCreativePenn.com
joanna@TheCreativePenn.com
Twitter: @thecreativepenn
Facebook.com/TheCreativePenn
YouTube.com/thecreativepenn
Instagram.com/JFPennAuthor

Appendix 1:
Bibliography

I've referred to a lot of books. You can find them all listed below. You can also download this at:

www.TheCreativePenn.com/nonfictiondownload

* * *

Art and Fear: Observations on the Perils (and Rewards) of Artmaking – David Bayles and Ted Orland

Bird by Bird: Some Instructions on Writing and Life
– Anne Lamott

Big Magic: Creative Living Beyond Fear
– Elizabeth Gilbert

Body of Work: Finding the Thread that Ties Your Story Together – Pamela Slim

Business for Authors: How to be an Author Entrepreneur
– Joanna Penn

Business for Punks: Break All The Rules
– The Brewdog Way - James Watt

Choosing A Self-Publishing Service
– Alliance of Independent Authors

Closing the Deal…On Your Terms: Agents, Contracts, and Other Considerations – Kristine Kathryn Rusch

How to Write a Book Proposal, 5th Edition
– Jody Rein & Michael Larsen

How to Write a Non-Fiction Book in 21 days
– That Readers Love! - Steve Scott

How to Write a Sizzling Synopsis – Bryan Cohen

I Could Do Anything If Only I Knew What It Was
– Barbara Sher

If You Want To Write: A Book About Art, Independence
and Spirit – Brenda Ueland

Juicy Pens, Thirsty Paper: Gifting the World with Your
Words and Stories, and Creating the Time and Energy
to Actually Do It – SARK

Make Good Art – Neil Gaiman

On Writing: A Memoir of the Craft – Stephen King

On Writing Well – William Zinsser

Perennial Seller: The Art of Making and Marketing Work
that Lasts – Ryan Holiday

Public Speaking for Authors, Creatives and Other
Introverts – Joanna Penn

Quiet: The Power of Introverts in a World That Can't Stop
Talking – Susan Cain

Resilience: Facing Down Rejection and Criticism on the
Road to Success – Mark McGuinness

Rich Dad, Poor Dad: What the Rich Teach Their Kids
About Money That the Poor and Middle Class Do Not!
– Robert Kiyosaki

Rise of the Youpreneur: The Definitive Guide to Becoming the Go-To Leader in Your Industry and Building a Future-Proof Business – Chris Ducker

Steal Like An Artist: 10 Things Nobody Told You About Being Creative – Austin Kleon

Story: Substance, Structure, Style and the Principles of Screenwriting – Robert McKee

Storynomics: Story-Driven Marketing in the Post-Advertising World – Robert McKee

Story Driven: You Don't Need to Compete When You Know Who You Are – Bernadette Jiwa

Successful Self-Publishing: How to Self-Publish and Market Your Book – Joanna Penn

The Art of Memoir – Mary Carr

The Business of Being a Writer – Jane Friedman

The Chicago Manual of Style – University of Chicago Press

The Compound Effect: Jumpstart Your Income, Your Life, Your Success – Darren Hardy

The Copyright Handbook: What Every Writer Needs to Know – Stephen Fishman

The Gifts of Imperfection: Let Go Of Who You Think You're Supposed To Be And Embrace Who You Are – Brené Brown

The Healthy Writer: Reduce Your Pain, Improve Your Health, and Build a Writing Career for the Long-Term – Joanna Penn and Dr Euan Lawson

The Million Dollar, One-Person Business: Make Great Money. Work the Way You Like. Have the Life You Want – Elaine Pofeldt

The New Rules of Marketing and PR: How to Use Social Media, Online Video, Mobile Applications, Blogs, News Releases, and Viral Marketing to Reach Buyers Directly – David Meerman Scott

The Pursuit of Perfection and How it Harms Writers – Kristine Kathryn Rusch

The Self-Publisher's Legal Handbook – Helen Sedwick

The Story Grid: What Good Editors Know – Shawn Coyne

The Successful Author Mindset: A Handbook for Surviving the Writer's Journey – Joanna Penn

The Writer's Guide to Training your Dragon – Scott Baker

Unshakeable: Your Guide to Financial Freedom – Tony Robbins

Vlog Like a Boss: How to Kill It Online with Video Blogging – Amy Schmittauer

Write to Market: Deliver a Book that Sells – Chris Fox

Writing Down the Bones: Freeing the Writer Within – Natalie Goldberg

You Must Write a Book: Boost Your Brand, Get More Business, and Become The Go-To Expert – Honorée Corder

Appendix 2:
Resources by Chapter

I've included a lot of references in the book and listed them all here. You can also download this at:

www.TheCreativePenn.com/nonfictiondownload

* * *

1.1 Why write a non-fiction book?

On Writing: A Memoir of the Craft – Stephen King

Big Magic: Creative Living Beyond Fear – Elizabeth Gilbert

Seth Godin's advice for authors: www.sethgodin.typepad. com/seths_blog/2006/08/advice_for_auth.html

How to Make a Living with your Writing: Books, Blogging, and More – Joanna Penn

The Successful Author Mindset: A Handbook for Surviving the Writer's Journey – Joanna Penn

Perennial Seller: The Art of Making and Marketing Work That Lasts – Ryan Holiday

1.2 Can I write a book if I'm not an expert?

Juicy Pens, Thirsty Paper: Gifting the World with Your Words and Stories, and Creating the Time and Energy to Actually Do It – SARK

If You Want To Write: A Book About Art, Independence and Spirit – Brenda Ueland

Make Good Art – Neil Gaiman

1.3 Originality. Or "there are already so many books on the topic"

Steal Like An Artist: 10 Things Nobody Told You About Being Creative – Austin Kleon

Big Magic: Creative Living Beyond Fear – Elizabeth Gilbert

1.4 Who are you? Personal stories and your writer's voice

How to Write a Non-Fiction Book in 21 days – That Readers Love! – Steve Scott

Writing Down the Bones: Freeing the Writer Within - Natalie Goldberg

Bird by Bird: Some Instructions on Writing and Life – Anne Lamott

1.5 Fear and self-doubt

The Successful Author Mindset: A Handbook for Surviving the Writer's Journey – Joanna Penn

Art and Fear: Observations on the Perils (and Rewards) of Artmaking – David Bayles and Ted Orland

2.1 Types of non-fiction books

Shawn Coyne on The Story Grid blog. Breakdown of non-fiction genres: www.storygrid.com/nonfictions-big-genre-silos

The Story Grid: What Good Editors Know – Shawn Coyne

2.2 Business models for non-fiction books

The Million Dollar, One-Person Business: Make Great Money. Work the Way You Like. Have the Life you Want – Elaine Pofeldt

How to Make a Living with your Writing: Books, Blogging, and More – Joanna Penn

Business for Authors: How to be an Author Entrepreneur – Joanna Penn

The Business of Being a Writer – Jane Friedman

How to Make Real Money Selling Books (Without Worrying About Returns) – Brian Jud

Public Speaking for Authors, Creatives and Other Introverts – Joanna Penn

You Must Write a Book: Boost Your Brand, Get More Business, and Become The Go-To Expert – Honorée Corder

2.3 Who is your book for? Identify your target market

Business for Punks: Break All the Rules – The Brewdog Way – James Watt

Seth Godin. Advice for authors: www.sethgodin.typepad.com/seths_blog/2006/08/advice_for_auth.html

K-lytics genre/niche reports:
www.TheCreativePenn.com/genre

KDP Rocket for category and keyword research:
www.TheCreativePenn.com/rocket

2.4 Decide on the topic for your book

Draft No. 4: On the Writing Process – John McPhee

Write to Market: Deliver a Book that Sells – Chris Fox

K-lytics genre/niche reports:
www.TheCreativePenn.com/genre

KDP Rocket for category and keyword research: www.TheCreativePenn.com/rocket

2.5 Decide on your book title

KDP Rocket for category and keyword research:
www.TheCreativePenn.com/rocket

PickFu for book title/cover testing:
www.TheCreativePenn.com/pickfubook

2.9 Your perspective on time

Perennial Seller: The Art of Making and Marketing Work that Lasts – Ryan Holiday

Big Magic: Creative Living Beyond Fear – Elizabeth Gilbert

2.10 Writing a book proposal

How to Write a Book Proposal, 5th Edition
– Jody Rein & Michael Larsen

Round-up of resources on book proposals from Jane Friedman: www.JaneFriedman.com/start-here-how-to-write-a-book-proposal

3.1 Gather and organize existing material

Scrivener software for organizing research, planning, writing and formatting: www.LiteratureAndLatte.com

Evernote app for organization: www.Evernote.com

3.2 Research, interviews, surveys and social listening

Interview with Ryan Holiday on his non-fiction process: www.TheCreativePenn.com/ryan1

Interview with Steven Pressfield on his research process for *The Lion's Gate*, mental toughness and Resistance: www.TheCreativePenn.com/pressfield1

Google Forms: docs.google.com/forms

Survey Monkey: www.SurveyMonkey.com

3.3 Structure and organize the book

Scrivener software for organizing research, planning, writing and formatting: www.LiteratureAndLatte.com

3.4 How to write the first draft

Google Calendar for scheduling time blocks: www.google.com/calendar

BOSE noise-cancelling headphones. Pricey but worth it. I wear them every time I write now, even when dictating. My link: www.TheCreativePenn.com/silence

Freedom app: www.freedom.to

Scrivener software for organizing research, planning, writing and formatting: www.LiteratureAndLatte.com

3.5 How to dictate your book

Nuance Dragon speech-to-text software:
www.TheCreativePenn.com/dragonsoftware

Blue Yeti microphone: www.TheCreativePenn.com/
blueyeti

Hand-held MP3 recorder. Sony ICD-PX333:
www.TheCreativePenn.com/sony

Dictate your Book – Monica Leonelle

The Writer's Guide to Training your Dragon – Scott Baker

Foolproof Dictation – Christopher Downing

Interview with Monica Leonelle on *How to Dictate your Book*: www.TheCreativePenn.com/monicadictate

Interview with Scott Baker on *How to Use Dictation to Write Faster and Stay Healthy*: www.TheCreativePenn.com/scott

3.6 Turn your blog/podcast/videos into a book

Example of evergreen article and video based on a chapter from *The Successful Author Mindset*: www.TheCreative-Penn.com/how-do-you-find-the-time-to-write

How to Blog a Book: Write, Publish, and Promote Your Work One Post at a Time – Nina Amir

3.7 Speed, quality and perfectionism

The Pursuit of Perfection and How it Harms Writers –
Kristine Kathryn Rusch

Article on writing fast and its relationship to quality by
prolific author, Dean Wesley Smith -
www.DeanWesleySmith.com/killing-the-sacred-cows-of-
publishing-writing-fast

3.9 Writer's block

Bird by Bird: Some Instructions on Writing and Life –
Anne Lamott

*Conquering Writer's Block and Summoning Inspiration:
Learn to Nurture a Lifestyle of Creativity* – K.M. Weiland

Interview on *How to Banish Writer's Block* with
K.M.Weiland on The Creative Penn Podcast: www.
TheCreativePenn.com/weiland

3.10 Co-writing a non-fiction book

*Co-Writing a Book: Collaboration and Co-creation for
Authors* – Joanna Penn and J. Thorn

Chapter on collaborations in *The Self-Publisher's Legal
Handbook* – Helen Sedwick

Article on co-writing mistakes:
www.TheCreativePenn.com/cowriting-mistakes

Interview with J. Thorn on co-writing:
www.TheCreativePenn.com/co-writing

Interview with Dr Euan Lawson on being a healthy writer and how we co-wrote *The Healthy Writer*: www.TheCreativePenn.com/healthy-cowriting

Interview with Emily Thompson on co-writing *Being Boss*: www.TheCreativePenn.com/beingboss

3.11 How to turn a boring book into an engaging read

My tutorial on using Grammarly: www.TheCreativePenn.com/grammarly-tutorial

Find freelancers at www.TheCreativePenn.com/pressfield1

If You Want to Write – Brenda Ueland

3.13 Does non-fiction have to be true?

The Art of Memoir – Mary Carr

3.14 Legal issues: Using real people, quotes, lyrics, images and citing sources

The Self-Publisher's Legal Handbook – Helen Sedwick

The Copyright Handbook: What Every Writer Needs to Know – Stephen Fishman

Closing the Deal...On Your Terms: Agents, Contracts, and Other Considerations – Kristine Kathryn Rusch

How to use Memorable Lyrics without Paying a Fortune or a Lawyer – Helen Sedwick and Jessica M. Brown

How to use Eye-Catching Images without Paying a Fortune or a Lawyer – Helen Sedwick and Jessica Brown

The Chicago Manual of Style – University of Chicago Press

Grammarly plagiarism checker and editing software: www.TheCreativePenn.com/grammarly

Legal issues blog for writers: www.HelenSedwick.com

Creative Law Center: www.CreativeLawCenter.com

Interview with attorney, Helen Sedwick, on copyright, publishing contract clauses, image use, and avoiding getting sued: www.TheCreativePenn.com/helen

3.15 Self-editing a book

Grammarly editing software: www.TheCreativePenn.com/grammarly

My Grammarly tutorial: www.TheCreativePenn.com/grammarly-tutorial

On Writing Well – William Zinsser

3.16 How to find and work with professional editors and proofreaders

My list of recommended editors:
www.TheCreativePenn.com/editors

My tutorial video on how to find and work with professional editors: www.TheCreativePenn.com/how-to-find-and-work-with-professional-editors

4.1 Your publishing options

Closing the Deal on your Terms: Agents, Contracts and Other Considerations – Kristine Katherine Rusch

How Authors Sell Publishing Rights – Orna Ross and Helen Sedwick

Successful Self-Publishing: How to Self-Publish and Market Your Book – Joanna Penn

Choosing A Self-Publishing Service – The Alliance of Independent Authors

The Alliance of Independent Authors Watchdog listing of publishing companies:
www.TheCreativePenn.com/watchdog

Find out more about the Alliance of Independent Authors: www.TheCreativePenn.com/alliance

Interview with Steven Spatz, CEO of BookBaby about self-publishing options:
www.TheCreativePenn.com/stevenspatz

You can get 10% off at BookBaby if you use my link: www.TheCreativePenn.com/bookbaby or just go to BookBaby.com

4.2 Use different formats to create multiple streams of income

Successful Self-Publishing: How to Self-Publish and Market Your Book – Joanna Penn

Tutorial on how to format ebooks and print books with Vellum: www.TheCreativePenn.com/format-ebook-print-with-vellum

Find out more on Vellum software: www.TheCreativePenn.com/vellum

Interview with Chris Ducker on *Rise of the Youpreneur* which goes into his non-fiction business model and how he produced his books as an independent: www.TheCreativePenn.com/ducker

Video: How to turn your book into a workbook: www.TheCreativePenn.com/workbook

Interview with John Lee Dumas on creating The Mastery Journal: www.TheCreativePenn.com/johnleedumas

Interview with Joel Friedlander on creating the Write Well journal: www.TheCreativePenn.com/writewell

How to self-publish your own audiobook: www.TheCreativePenn.com/how-to-self-publish-an-audiobook

How to record your own audiobook: www.TheCreativePenn.com/record-audiobooks-acx

4.3 Non-fiction book covers

My list of professional book cover designers:
www.TheCreativePenn.com/bookcoverdesign

www.TheBookDesigner.com has cover design awards
every month so you can check out other designers

Video tutorial of the design process: www.TheCreative-
Penn.com/find-and-work-with-a-book-cover-designer

4.4 Book formatting for non-fiction: Tables, images, graphical elements

Free formatting options and a list of professionals:
www.TheCreativePenn.com/formatting

Vellum software for formatting ebooks and print:
www.TheCreativePenn.com/vellum

My tutorial on how to format for ebook and print here:
www.TheCreativePenn.com/format-ebook-print-with-
vellum

The Chicago Manual of Style – University of Chicago Press

4.5 Pricing your book

How to Market a Book – Joanna Penn

*Discoverability: Help Readers Find You In Today's World of
Publishing* – Kristine Kathryn Rusch

4.6 Your book sales description

Interview with Bryan Cohen, author of *How to Write a Sizzling Synopsis*, on The Creative Penn podcast: www.TheCreativePenn.com/bryancohen

Amazon Author Central for the US store: authorcentral. amazon.com Also available for the UK and other country stores.

Author Marketing Club's Enhanced Description Maker, part of their premium service: www.TheCreativePenn.com/amc

4.7 Categories and keywords

K-lytics for niche and category research - www.TheCreativePenn.com/genre

KDP Rocket for keyword and category research - www.TheCreativePenn.com/rocket

4.8 Turn your non-fiction book into a multimedia course

Teachable is my recommended course hosting platform: www.TheCreativePenn.com/teachable

Screenflow for Mac: www.telestream.net/screenflow

Camtasia for PC: www.techsmith.com/video-editor.html

Blue Yeti microphone: www.TheCreativePenn.com/blueyeti

Skype for recording interviews: www.Skype.com

ECamm Call Recorder for Skype (Mac):
www.ecamm.com/mac/callrecorder/

Pamela call recorder for PC: www.pamela.biz

Audacity audio software: www.audacityteam.org

How to Write Non-Fiction Multimedia Course: www.
TheCreativePenn.com/writenonfiction

* * *

For more detail on how to build an online course, check
out the free *Course Creation Toolkit Bundle* by Joseph
Michael, the Scrivener Coach, who has made multi-six-
figures from his Learn Scrivener Fast course:
www.TheCreativePenn.com/coursecreation

4.9 Updating your books over time

*Successful Self-Publishing: How to Self-Publish and Market
Your Book* – Joanna Penn

Seth Godin's article on updating *All Marketers are
Liars*: http://sethgodin.typepad.com/all_market-
ers_are_liars/2009/11/a-new-cover-a-new-foreword-but-
the-same-book.html

5.1 Two models of marketing and the importance of mindset

How to Market a Book – Joanna Penn

5.2 Book-centered marketing

Perennial Seller: The Art of Making and Marketing Work that Lasts – Ryan Holiday

Write to Market: Deliver a Book That Sells – Chris Fox

5.3 Paid advertising for non-fiction books

Amazon Marketing Services for the US Amazon store: ams.amazon.com

KDP Rocket for keyword research: www.TheCreativePenn.com/rocket

BookBub Featured Deals and Ads: partners.bookbub.com

Go direct to Kobo Writing Life and request access to the Promotions tab: www.Kobo.com/writinglife

Help! My Facebook Ads Suck: Simple Steps to Turn Those Ads Around – Michael Cooper

Mastering Amazon Ads: An Author's Guide – Brian D. Meeks

* * *

If you'd like a comprehensive course, I recommend Mark Dawson's *Advertising for Authors*. You can sign up for the waitlist at: www.TheCreativePenn.com/ads

5.4 Author-centered marketing. The power of a personal brand

Rise of the Youpreneur: The Definitive Guide to Becoming the Go-To Leader in Your Industry and Building a Future-Proof Business – Chris Ducker

The Gifts of Imperfection: Let Go Of Who You Think You're Supposed To Be And Embrace Who You Are – Brené Brown

The Successful Author Mindset: A Handbook for Surviving the Writer's Journey – Joanna Penn

5.5 Build your author website

Tutorial on how to build your own author website in under 30 minutes: www.TheCreativePenn.com/authorwebsite

Tutorial on how to set up the Author Pro WordPress Theme: www.TheCreativePenn.com/setup-author-pro-theme

5.6 Build an email list

Tutorial on setting up your email list signup:
www.TheCreativePenn.com/setup-email-list

ConvertKit email service:
www.TheCreativePenn.com/convert

Sign up for the Author 2.0 Blueprint:
www.TheCreativePenn.com/blueprint

ConvertKit GDPR guidelines:
www.TheCreativePenn.com/GDPR

5.7 Integrate email marketing with your book

Interview with Joseph Alexander on his print-focused
publishing model and email funnel:
www.TheCreativePenn.com/joseph

Direct sales platforms: Selz.com, PayHip.com,
PayPal direct, Shopify.com

Delivery of ebook to customer's device:
www.BookFunnel.com

Automation service: zapier.com

5.8 Content marketing for non-fiction books

The New Rules of Marketing and PR: How to Use Social Media, Online Video, Mobile Applications, Blogs, News Releases, and Viral Marketing to Reach Buyers Directly – David Meerman Scott

The Creative Penn Blog: www.TheCreativePenn.com/blog

The Creative Penn YouTube channel: www.YouTube.com/thecreativepenn

Social Warfare plugin for WordPress: www.warfareplugins.com

Wired article on podcasting, Jan 2018: www.wired.com/story/apple-podcast-analytics-first-month

Transcription service: www.speechpad.com

The Creative Penn Podcast subscription and over 370 backlist episodes: www.TheCreativePenn.com/podcast

Vlog Like a Boss: How to Kill It Online with Video Blogging – Amy Schmittauer

Inc article on video marketing: https://www.inc.com/gordon-tredgold/20-reasons-why-you-should-boost-your-video-marketing-budget-in-2017.html

Forbes article on video marketing: https://www.forbes.com/sites/forbesagencycouncil/2017/02/03/video-marketing-the-future-of-content-marketing/#139365016b53

Image creation for social sharing: www.canva.com

5.9 My non-fiction marketing journey

My favorite sites for professional bloggers:
Entrepreneurs-Journey.com, Problogger.com,
Copyblogger.com

Yaro Starak's up-to-date Blog Profits Blueprint at:
www.TheCreativePenn.com/blogblueprint

Wayback Machine Internet Archives:
http://archive.org/web/

My tutorial on how to build your own website at:
www.TheCreativePenn.com/authorwebsite

The Compound Effect: Jumpstart Your Income, Your Life, Your Success – Darren Hardy

My video on the international Kindle from 2009:
www.TheCreativePenn.com/international_kindle

How to Market a Book – Joanna Penn

How to Make a Living with your Writing – Joanna Penn

Other Books by Joanna Penn

Get your FREE Successful Author Blueprint
and video series:

www.TheCreativePenn.com/blueprint

More Books for Writers

How to Make a Living with Your Writing:
Books, Blogging and More

Successful Self-Publishing:
How to publish an ebook and a print book

How to Market a Book

The Successful Author Mindset

Public Speaking for Authors,
Creatives, and Other Introverts

Co-Writing a Book: Collaboration and
Co-creation for Writers

Business for Authors: How to be an Author Entrepreneur

Career Change: Stop Hating your Job, Discover
What you Really Want to Do, and Start Doing It

* * *

Thrillers by J.F.PENN

Get a free thriller: www.JFPenn.com/free

ARKANE Thrillers

Stone of Fire #1
Crypt of Bone #2
Ark of Blood #3
One Day in Budapest #4
Day of the Vikings #5
Gates of Hell #6
One Day in New York #7
Destroyer of Worlds #8
End of Days #9

London Crime Thrillers

Desecration #1
Delirium #2
Deviance #3

Mapwalker Dark Fantasy series

Map of Shadows #1

Standalone Fantasy Thrillers

Risen Gods - with J.Thorn

A Thousand Fiendish Angels:
Short Stories Inspired by Dante's Inferno

The Dark Queen:
An Archaeological Short Story

American Demon Hunters: Sacrifice
- with J. Thorn, Lindsay Buroker, Zach Bohannon

Acknowledgements

Thank you to my audience at The Creative Penn. Your support enables me to continue the journey of being a creative entrepreneur.

Thanks to everyone who completed my survey about writing non-fiction. Special thanks to those quoted in the book: Dr Karen Wyatt, Leeza Baric, and Ali Luke.

Thanks to Jane Dixon Smith at JD Smith Design for the book cover and interior print design, to Liz Dexter at LibroEditing for proofreading, and to Alexandra Amor for beta reading and double-checking attributions.

Made in the USA
Las Vegas, NV
20 December 2021

39022217R00203